A KNIGHT AND HIS CASTLE

D0033945

By the same author:
A KNIGHT AND HIS ARMOUR
A KNIGHT AND HIS HORSE
A KNIGHT AND HIS WEAPONS
A KNIGHT IN BATTLE
DARK AGE WARRIOR
THE ARCHAEOLOGY OF WEAPONS
THE SWORD IN THE AGE OF CHIVALRY

About the Author

Ewart Oakeshott was born in 1916. He began collecting swords while still in school at Dulwich, and has since built up a superb collection, specializing in the medieval period. His books include *The Archaeology of Weapons, European Weapons and Armour,* and *The Sword in the Age of Chivalry.* His books for children include the acclaimed 'Knight' series, of which this book, *The Knight and His Castle* was the first. He always brings to his books a wide and deep knowledge of his subject, and a witty and pithy style. The *Times Educational Supplement* rightly called him "one of those rarely gifted researchers who combine exhaustive investigation with absorbing enthusiasm." Oakeshott (and three friends) founded the Arms and Armour Society, a flourishing concern with a worldwide membership. His home is in Ely, close to Cambridge, England.

A KNIGHT
AND HIS CASTLE

Second Edition

EWART OAKESHOTT F.S.A.
Illustrated by the author

Dufour Editions

First published 1966,
this revised second edition published 1997

Published in the United States of America by
Dufour Editions Inc., Chester Springs, Pennsylvania, 19425

Library of Congress Cataloguing-in-Publication Data:
Oakeshott, R. Ewart.
    A knight and his castle / R. Ewart Oakeshott : illustrated
by the author. — 2nd ed.
        p.   cm.
    Includes index.
    Summary: Traces the design, building, and defense of
castles throughout medieval Europe, and describes the
daily life of a knight.
    ISBN-0-8023-1294-2 (pbk.)
    1. Knights and knighthood—Juvenile literature.
2. Chivalry—Juvenile literature. 3. Castles—Juvenile
literature. 4. Civilization, Medieval—Juvenile literature.
[1. Knights and knighthood. 2. Chivalry. 3. Castles.
4. Civilization, Medieval.]
I. Title.
CR4513.02   1993
909.07—dc20   93-2210
                                                        CIP
                                                         AC

ISBN 0 8023 1294 2

Printed and bound in the United States of America

Contents

Earl Richard of Warwick

One of the most splendid effigies of a knight that you could ever wish to see is in St. Mary's Church in Warwick, England. It is made of bronze, gilded; it really looks just like a man in golden armor, so lifelike is the face and so carefully accurate in detail the armor. Every bit of this, on the back as well as the front, is most carefully made; not a strap or buckle, not a rivet is missing. There is a sword on the left side; on the right there used to be a dagger, but this, being easily hidden, has long since been stolen, as have the pair of gauntlets that once lay beside the sword. The knight's head rests upon a great jousting helm crested with a swan, and at his feet is a bear.

The effigy was made in 1454, and is a lifelike portrait of the man whose body lies in the tomb-chest underneath it. His name was Richard Beauchamp, Earl of Warwick, and five hundred years ago his home was in a castle that still stands a little way outside the town of Warwick, and is still lived in just as it was in his lifetime. He was a real man, whose effigy is certainly the work of a great artist and the finest example in the world of sculptured armor. But look at the face of the man himself: would you think that this was a warrior, a tremendous swordsman and jouster, one of the leading captains of his day? More likely, if he wasn't clad in full armor, you might imagine that he was a thinker, a man of law, perhaps, or a writer, or an artist. We know a lot about his deeds, though — real, splendid feats of arms worthy of a Sir Lancelot.

Long after his death, and after his more famous son-in-law, Warwick the King-maker, had been slain at the battle of Barnet in 1471, an elderly historian called John Rous, who had served these two Earls all his life, inspired one of his assistants to write a record of the deeds of Earl Richard. He called his book *A Pageant of the Birth, Life and Death of Richard Beauchamp, Earl of Warwick.* He had intended it to be a book of pictures with a little text, like a caption, on each page. A Flemish painter was commissioned to do the pictures, but the work was never finished. Only the text and the rough sketches for the paintings were done. These sketches as we can see them today look just like pencil drawings, but of course they are not, because pencils as we know them were not in use at the end of the 15th century. They were done with an instrument called a plummet, a sort of stick of lead pointed at one end which made a mark exactly like a 'lead' pencil does — except that the lead of a pencil is not really made of lead at all, but graphite. Many years after the *Pageant* was left unfinished, the 17th-century historian Dugdale rewrote it,

The effigy of Richard Beauchamp, Earl of Warwick, in the Beauchamp Chapel in the Church of St. Mary, Warwick. It is made of bronze, thickly gilded, and shows a Milanese armor of about 1450.

though he added little or nothing to it. He simply modernized the spelling; I have done the same here, modernizing Dugdale's spelling in some of the most interesting bits I have taken to tell of Earl Richard's life.

He was born, heir to one of the greatest titles in the realm, on January 25, 1381. At his christening his godfathers were the King — Richard II — and the Archbishop of Canterbury, so you can see what an important baby he was. We hear little about him until he was nineteen, when he was made a Knight of the Bath by Henry IV in 1400. Then begins the long tale of his deeds of arms. At the coronation of Henry IV's new queen, Joan of Navarre, in 1401, Richard Beauchamp "kept justice in the Queen's part, against all comers, wherein he behaved himself most nobly." This means that at one of the tournaments held in celebration, he challenged everyone who cared to joust with him as the Queen's Champion, and he did very well. The same way, in a more warlike manner, "he was retained to serve the King for one year with 100 men at arms and 300 archers." This was because he was one of the chief barons of the realm and had to maintain a band of trained fighting men to serve the King when he needed them. And two years later, in 1403, need them he did, for he had to face the forces of the rebellious Earls of Northumberland and Westmoreland, led by Northumberland's son Henry Percy, the famous Hotspur. Earl Richard fought at the battle of Shrewsbury with the King and the young Prince of Wales (afterwards Henry V) and after the battle he was made a Knight of the Garter.

Five years later, in 1408, he got leave of the King to travel and visit the Holy Land "for performance of a vow he had made, and pilgrimage he resolved to take. He fitted himself with all necessaries for that journey, and passed the sea. In which voyage, visiting his cousin the Duke of Bar, he was nobly received and entertained by him for six days; who then accompanied him to Paris, where being arrived, the King of France then wearing his crown in reverence of that holy feast, made him to sit at his table." (Kings in the Middle Ages wore their crowns ceremonially during the feasts of Christmas, Easter, and Pentecost.) "And at his departure, sent a herald to conduct him safely through that realm of France."

"Out of which, entering Lombardy, he was met by another herald from a knight called Sir Pandulf Malacet, with a challenge to perform certain feats of arms with him at Verona, upon a day assigned and in the presence of Sir Galeot of Mantua; wherunto he gave his assent. And as soon as he had performed his pilgrimage at Rome returned to Verona, where he and his opponent were first to joust, next, to fight with axes, afterwards with arming swords, and lastly with sharp daggers. At the day and place assigned for such exercises, came great resort of people, Sir Pandulf entering the lists with nine spears borne before him. The Act of Spears being ended, they fell to it with axes, in which encounter Sir Pandulf got a sore wound in the shoulder and would have been utterly slain, had not Sir Galeot cried 'Peace'.

"From thence he travelled to Venice; where being nobly received by the Duke (the Doge) and others, he had many great presents given to him by reason of the honor he had gained at Verona." Next he went on to Jerusalem, and back to Venice again. Then he visited Russia, Lithuania, Poland, Prussia, Westphalia, and parts of Germany, "showing great valor in various tournaments."

He was back in England again in 1412, so he had travelled all these distances and visited all the lands — and fought in them — in the space of only four years.

As soon as Earl Richard returned to England, he was "by an Indenture of 2nd October 1412 retained with Henry, Prince of Wales, to serve him in peace and war, both in this realm and on and beyond the seas, for 250 marks per annum, to be paid out of the Prince's exchequer at Carmarthen at Easter and Michaelmas, in two even portions. And wherever he should be in that prince's court to have four esquires and six yeomen with him, and diet there for them all. Provided, that the Prince, in service of war, should have the third part of what he got in battle, and the third part of the thirds his men-at-arms should gain; and in case he took any great commander, port, or castle, the Prince likewise to have them, giving him reasonable satisfaction."

This tells us a good deal about one of the jobs a great landowner in the 15th century had to do.

Barons like Earl Richard were not just luxury-loving millionaires, forever hunting and feasting and going to tournaments. They had important parts to play in the conduct and government of the country in peacetime and in the organization of its forces in war. This particular job, which the Earl was given when he got home, had more to do with military affairs than with the business of government. But what exactly does it mean, that he was 'retained' by an 'Indenture'? A medieval indenture was a legal document, like a contract. Two copies were written on a single sheet of parchment, one copy on the top part of the sheet and the other on the bottom part. The two halves were then separated across the center by cutting the sheet in an 'indented' or wavy line; one copy was then kept by each of the contracting parties. In this way there could never be any doubt about the two parts belonging together; nobody could forge a copy or make a false one, since it would be impossible to copy the wavy line of cutting accurately. The two halves had to join exactly when they were brought together.

To be 'retained' simply meant that one was given a job to do for somebody — just as a history teacher is appointed to a school to serve under a principal, and as the principal is himself appointed to serve the local education authority. Earl Richard was given a post under the Prince of Wales, and to fill it properly he was required to have four squires and six yeomen with him all the time. A yeoman was usually some sort of fighting man, not of knightly rank but with some other 'trade,' like an engineer in the Army. He might have been an armorer or a farrier (a man who looked after the horses) or a cook for example. We can be sure that each of these yeoman was a specialist, a tradesman in modern terms, in some particular and important way.

The Earl was paid 250 marks a year for this service. A mark was two-thirds of a pound sterling. A mark in 1412 would have been worth about $350 in modern values, so the total of his salary would have been about $90,000 per year — good pay; but of course out of it he had to pay his squires and yeoman "and diet for them all" — in other words, he had to feed them as well. This salary wasn't paid to him every month, but twice a year, about $45,000 at Easter and the same again at *Michaelmas*. A condition of this service was that in the time of war the Earl had to hand over one-third of the loot or ransom-money he himself got in battle; if his squires or yeoman took any spoils or prisoners, *they* handed over two-thirds of their takings to the Earl their master, and one-third of the third they had left they had to pay over to the Prince. If the Earl or his men made a very important capture — an enemy commander, port or castle — it was at once given to the Prince, who would pay a suitable compensation.

In 1413, the following year, Prince Henry became King Henry V, and at his coronation Earl Richard was made High Steward of England, a very important office indeed. In the same year he crossed the Channel to see if there was any possibility of making a firm and lasting peace with France and to discuss the idea of a marriage between Henry V and the King of France's daughter, Katherine. This embassy failed, and within a few months England and France were at war again.

On the outbreak of this war in 1415, Earl Richard was made captain of Calais, one of the key military commands in wartime. He was 34 years old, and now we can see the change in his staff. When he had his previous job in 1412, with his four squires and his six yeoman, he was just a member of the Prince's household. Now he was himself a high-ranking general with his own retinue of thirty men-at-arms and thirty mounted archers, two hundred foot soldiers and two hundred archers on foot. This was for peacetime. In war this increased to one hundred forty men-at-arms, one hundred fifty mounted archers, one hundred foot soldiers, one hundred eighty four archers on foot and four scouts on horseback as well as forty crossbowmen, twenty carpenters, five masons and armorers, bowyers, fletchers, *farriers*, other officers, and pensioners, "for which service he was to receive himself 6/8d. a day, for his knights 2/- a day apiece, for the rest of his horse 1/-; for every mounted archer and every foot soldier, 8d., and for every archer on foot 6d. a day for their wages." So he got about $175.00 a day in modern values, his knights about $50.00, his troopers about $30.00, his mounted archers and foot soldiers about $20.00 and his foot-archers about $15.00.

When he arrived at Calais to take up his appointment, he found that the French did not seem likely to attack the town at all, and decided instead to devise a tournament. Although I have said a good deal about tournaments in another book, it will be worth while here to describe this one, for the arranging and organizing of tournaments was one of the most notable functions of the lord of a castle or the governor of a city.

"He caused three shields to be made, one for a Green Knight, one for a Chevalier Vert, and one for a knight he called the Chevalier Attendant; all three must run a course with sharp spears. Each made out a challenge, which was sent to the court of the King of France. Three French knights took up the challenges and agreed to meet at a day and place assigned, which was a land called the Park-Hedge of Guines. The first, Sir Gerard Herbaumes, called himself Chevalier Rouge; the second was Sir Hugh Launey, who called himself the Chevalier Blanc, and the third was Sir Collard Fines.

"On the appointed day, the Earl, impersonating the Green Knight, came into the field with his face covered, a plume of ostrich feathers in his helm, and his horse trapped with the Lord Toney's arms (one of his ancestors). When first encountering with the Chevalier Rouge, at the third course he unhorsed him and so returned with closed visor, unknown, to his pavilion whence he sent to the Red Knight a good courser.

"The next day he came into the field as the Chevalier Vert, with his visor closed, a chaplet on his helm and a plume of ostrich feathers aloft, his horse trapped with the arms of Hanslap, viz. Argent, two bars Gules, where he met with the Chevalier Blanc, with whom he encountered, smote off his visor thrice and broke his besagews and other harness and returned victoriously to his pavilion with all his own habiliments safe, and as yet not known to any; from which he sent this Chevalier Blanc (Sir Hugh Launey) a good courser.

"But the day after, the last day of the joust, he came with his face open and his helmet as the day before, save that the chaplet was rich with pearls and precious stones, and his coat of arms of Guy and Beauchamp quarterly, having the arms of Toney and Hanslap on his trappers, and said that as he had performed the service the two days before, so with God's grace he would the third. Whereupon, encountering with Sir Collard Fines, at every stroke he bore him backward on his horse, insomuch that the Frenchman said that he seemed to be bound to his saddle; the Earl, to disprove this, jumped off his horse and on again. But all being ended he returned to his pavilion, sent to Sir Collard Fines a fair courser, feasted all the people, gave to those three knights great rewards and so rode back to Calais with great honour."

The Earl served with great distinction in Henry V's campaigns in France, though in the *Pageant* nothing is said about his being at Agincourt. In 1420 he went again into France to arrange a marriage between the King and the Princess Katherine, but this time he went with 1,000 men-at-arms at his back, and as we know the marriage took place that same year.

Another source of interesting detail about some of his daily doings is in one of his Household Account books for the years 1431–32. It was in 1431 that little Henry VI, then 10 years old, came to France to be crowned in Paris; in the Earl's account book we find several references to this visit.

The first entry in the book is for the parchment and covers for making the book itself, and there are many others such as: "For 3 Loads of Rushes bought of Halshide for the chamber of the Lord and Lady, 23/- ." But more interesting are those referring to visits, such as: "Saturday, 23rd June. The King came, with 2 Dukes, 6 knights, 18 squires, and 20 yeoman to drink, and went away." "Monday, 6th August. The lord went away with 11 squires, 13 yeoman, 12 grooms, 8 pages, and 26 horses after breakfast. Also there came Madame Talbot with 1 damsel, 1 esquire, a Nun of Laen, William Norreys, Richard Beauchamp, Mr. John Upton to dinner and supper and went away." "Monday, 19th November. Of the marriage of James Dryland and Alice Lightfoot. There came Madame Talbot with 2 damsels and 4 squires to dinner and supper and the night. Also came the Earl of Stafford, Lord de Audley, Sir William Peyto and 10 esquires and 13 yeoman, also James Dryland with 8 grooms, Madame Blont, Madame Peyto, Madame Godard with 8 damsels, 6 wives of burgesses of the city, Master John Upton, 4 of the king's yeomen of the crown to dinner and went away."

There are other entries in this book that are interesting because they tell us something about the way people travelled: "And in expenses of the Lady Countess of Warwick going by water from Rouen to Paris beginning on Saturday 1st. December, going by water and staying for 7 days and so to Friday on which day at night she entered Paris — with Madame Talbot, 2 damsels, 3 esquires, 1 groom, Madame Godard with 1 damsel, 2 yeomen, 1 page, 4 officers of the King, 1 esquire of the Cardinal with 1 yeoman, 2 armorers, with 54 persons, guests for the same time." "And for one 'Schonte' (a kind of barge) hired at Rouen carrying the Lord's gear and provisions, viz. wheat, oats and fish with firewood and other things, to Paris against the King's coronation...and to 15 barges hired for the barge of the Lord Duke of Bedford carrying the Lady Countess of Warwick with Lady Talbot and the damsels of the Lady with other damsels and with diverse officers of the King from Rouen to Paris against the King's coronation with 10/– paid for bridge tolls...and given by the hands of the Lord and Lady to the Master of the barge in reward for his labor going from Rouen to Paris — £8/5/– Tournois."

"And for 4 new wheels bought and made for the Lord's chariot with ironwork and nails and with the mending of the body of the said chariot together with the oversight by John Ball, with 4 traces bought for the same work. And for the making of 1 chariot of the Lord overseen by John Ball."

There are many more entries of a similar kind, which show that travelling by road in chariots, which were four-wheeled coaches of the kind that were still being used in the time of Charles I two hundred years later, was nearly as usual as travelling by water.

When John, Duke of Bedford, Regent of France, died in 1435, Earl Richard became Lieutenant-General of the whole realm of France — meaning of course the English bit of it, now much reduced, and what he could win back. The *Pageant* goes on: "Whereupon, with his lady and son taking shipping for the passage over, and discerning great danger by a hideous tempest, he caused himself, with both of them, to be bound to the main mast of the ship; to the intent that, if they perished and were after found yet by his coat of arms discovering who he was, they might be buried together." But they arrived safely in France. Here the historian, Dugdale, does add something of his own: "The state and lustre of his equipage in this journey may in some sort be discerned by his painter's bill..." A transcript of the bill follows, which shows how much work a painter retained by a great magnate had to do. Mostly it is the emblazoning of shields and banners, great *pennons* for the ships and pennants for the lances of his knights, all aglow with the vivid colors of his heraldry — the arms of Guy and Beauchamp and Hanslap, the repeated device of the Warwick Bear and Ragged Staff, and all the other arms and devices of his family and household.

When Richard died four years later in 1437, he was one of the most influential statesmen in the country, and a beloved military hero. He was 58 — not elderly by modern standards, but a good age in the 15th century. He died in Rouen, so his body had to be brought to Warwick castle for his funeral.

Richard Beauchamp's funeral must have been a very magnificent one, although his tomb was not ready. Indeed, the chapel that was being built to contain it was unfinished when he died. Not until six or seven years later was the chapel completed, and work on the tomb itself started. The tomb was designed by one of the chief masons of the time, John Essex, a 'marbler' (sculptor) of London. Much of the actual work on the tomb was done by John Brode, a marbler of Corfe in Dorset, who began work on it many years before it was finished in 1454. The furnishing of the chapel was undertaken by two more leading craftsmen, Prudde, the royal glazier who did the windows, and Richard Bird, carpenter of London, who made the carved desks with panelled backs, which are still there, and a screen for the organ.

All the figure-work, and there is much of it, was done by John Massingham, a worthy contemporary of Donatello and England's most eminent sculptor at this time. He carved the 'patterns' in wood for the small figures that stand in niches round the tombs sides — 'weepers' they called them — and in 1450 he began to make the life-sized portrait figure of the Earl in his armor to go on top. When the patterns

21

The head of Richard Beauchamp's effigy, a most beautifully sculptured portrait. The 'Pattern' for this figure was carved in wood by John Massingham. Unless it had been carved during his lifetime, the head would probably have been done from a death-mask of the Earl's face.

were finished, they went to London to Mr. William Austen, Coppersmith of London, who made molds from them, and cast the figures in bronze which was then gilded. Massingham was paid £66 — about $35,000 in modern values — between 1447 and 1449 for work he had done in this chapel, and we have the account for Austen's casting of the effigy.

You might wonder, when I say that this effigy is a portrait of the Earl, how it could be done accurately fifteen years after he was dead; he couldn't sit for John Massingham while he sculpted his face. The reason is that during the 14th and 15th centuries, and possibly before that as well, it was customary, when a great personage died, to make a cast in wax or plaster of his face. This was done to ensure that an absolutely correct portrait of the head could be added to the figure which, dressed in robes of state, would lie on top of the coffin during a lying-in-state or a funeral. In the museum in the cloisters at Westminster Abbey there are several of these "death-masks" of the medieval monarchs. The best are those of Edward III (died 1377), Anne of Bohemia, Richard II's queen (died 1393), and Henry VII (died 1507). If you compare these actual casts of the royal faces with the faces of their effigies up in the Abbey, you can see how the sculptor probably used the death-mask as a model. So it must have been with Earl Richard. Massingham would have carved his wooden figure with a death-mask of the Earl's face in front of him as a model. Before him, too, was a model for the armor. But what he used wasn't an old armor of the Earl's. He died, you remember, in 1439; Massingham was carving his figure in 1450-54. During these eleven years, the style of plate-armor had changed somewhat. This armor that we can see in St. Mary's Church is one that would have been absolutely up-to-date in 1450; there are several armors still surviving that we know could not have been made before this date, and in many Italian paintings done between 1445 and 1455 we see exactly similar armors.

Men such as John Essex, John Brode, and Richard Bird of London were those who worked on the great castles. Famous and eminent architects who designed the cathedrals and abbeys designed castles too — in consultation of course with military men who knew what they needed, like Richard Lion-Heart, who was himself a wonderful castle-designer, as well as a fighting man, a fine poet, and a writer of songs. But the castles, which were centers of culture and the homes of wealthy people, needed to be furnished. So in every age of castle-building the very best craftsmen and the finest artists would be commissioned to make the panelling in the chapel, the great hall, and the Lord's Solar and bedchamber, to do the glasswork in the windows of the hall and chapel, to make tapestries to cover the walls, and to paint those walls that were not to be panelled or hung with fabric. These castles were not forts; they were the homes of the rich and noble.

Castles, Squires, and Knights

When we stand under the walls of a medieval castle, we think of war. In imagination we hear the roar and hubbub of battle — the clash of steel, war-cries, the creak and clatter and thump of mangonels, the splintering impact of the stones they throw, the rhythmic, deadly thudding of battering-rams, the hiss of boiling oil poured from the battlements upon the warriors in the moat, the rattling hail of arrows. If we consider the inside of the castle, we tend to picture fierce barons, surrounded by a horde of soldiery, armed to the teeth, feasting and drinking deep in the castle hall, while miserable prisoners starve in rat-infested dungeons below, rotting in damp and filth. Such a picture, highly colored and based upon romantic ignorance, is all the more difficult to wipe away because there is a slight element of truth in it. There were sieges and ferocious fights below the walls. There were barons, though they were on the whole less fierce and more civilized than some stories would suggest. There were unhappy prisoners, too.

But let us try to see the castle as it really was. For every day of warfare the average English castle endured, there were thousands of days of peace. Many castles were never besieged at all. The significance of the medieval castle is in the fact that it was not just a fortress, it was the home of a family. From the castle all the business of the local government of a district was carried on, and to it came a constant stream of visitors — not only knightly folk, but artists, craftsmen, musicians, writers, and men of law. There would be the masons who were working on the great cathedrals and abbeys, for instance. These men, though they were called masons, were what we today would call architects. Many of them were very distinguished personages whose skill and advice were sought by monarchs — men who designed great and glorious buildings like the Angel Choir of Lincoln Cathedral, the Spire of Salisbury, Exeter nave, the great castles of Conway, Beaumaris, and Carnarvon. There would be sculptors, like John Massingham. Chaucer must have stayed at many castles, so must have Jean Froissart. These are men of the very highest quality: Chaucer, the great poet and story-teller, the admired friend of Richard II and his court; Froissart, a popular historian most rarely gifted — really more like a first-class historical novelist — a friend of Edward III's queen, Philippa of Hainault, and a companion of the Black Prince and all the great knights about whom he wrote so vividly. These, and their lesser known contemporaries, were the sort of men you might find in a castle. There would also be musicians, composers, instrumentalists, and singers — men such as today's James Galway, Yo-Yo Ma, and Luciano Pavarotti — and there were always the popular entertainers, in groups or singly, famous in their day as are the pop groups and singers now. Then there would be the great sportsmen — jousters, swordsmen, and men superlatively skilled in riding or *venery* — that is, hawking, hunting, and woodcraft generally, skills paralleled today in the show-jumping ring and on the race-track. There would be great Captains — William Marshal, Simon de Montfort, John Giffard, Henry of Grosmont, Earl of Derby, Thomas Dagworth, Robert Knollys — the list could be endless. Suppose we imagine a group of guests at dinner in the Great Hall at Warwick on a day in 1357. The Earl, Thomas Beauchamp, is at home. With him are several noblemen of France, captives he had taken when he commanded the right wing of the Black Prince's army at Poitiers the year before. There are also Mr. Henry Yevele, the great architect who is working on the plans for the new nave of Canterbury Cathedral; Sir Robert Knollys, a famous and popular captain of mercenaries, who is home on leave from France; an Abbess who is on her way to visit the King's court at Windsor; a group of musicians who have been asked to join the Prince's court at Bordeaux; a painter who is working on a series of murals in the Earl's apartments; and one of the Justices of the King's Bench with his retinue of clerks and officers. If you translate such a gathering into contemporary terms, you would have a great figure such

27

as a high-ranking government official as host, a group of corporate executives, a leading architect or artist, a general, a well-respected author, a well-known pop group, and a Supreme Court justice.

A castle was the place where such people, travel-

The Castle of Lusignan in France. This is drawn from a picture of the castle painted in about 1418; the castle was mostly built two hundred years earlier. This shows very well what a medieval castle looked like while it was still in use. The roofs were covered with red tiles, blue-grey slate, or stone slabs.

ling about on their affairs, would naturally stay, though of course they often stayed at abbeys as well. There would be other people as well, equally as interesting, who would have an even more direct and practical effect on the cultural life of the neighborhood. These were merchants and the travelling sales representatives of overseas manufacturers. Let us not imagine that the Commercial Traveller is a mod-

The great cylindrical tower in the middle of the castle, with its machicolated parapet and elaborate roof with many small gables and 'Tourelles' is later in date than the rest of the castle, and must have been quite new when the picture was painted. Adjoining it is the Great Hall and the domestic buildings.

ern character. His predecessors have been well established since the Bronze Age. Those who came to the medieval castles were the representatives of firms manufacturing or marketing luxury goods —

Venetians selling silk from China, or ivory, spices, or
confectionery from India and Africa, rich velvets
from Genoa and Florence, furs from Sweden or
Russia, cloth from Flanders, beautiful leather goods
from Cordova, wall-hangings from Arras, armor and
weapons from Milan, Augsburg, Innsbruck, and Bordeaux — and, of course, wine merchants from France
and Germany. To the castle folk, the armorers' representatives would probably have been the most
interesting, particularly the Milaners, for from Milan
came the best wares — so much so that the name
given in the 14th and 15th centuries to the travellers
has become the word 'milliner'. Armor was of course
the Milaners' principal product, but they carried
samples of all sorts of other goods as well — clothes,
hats, and fancy goods of all kinds. Big armorers'
firms like the Missaglia of Milan probably did a lot
of trade in men's outfitting, and may very well have
had great influence on the changes of fashion in
dress, as we know that they were the arbiters of
fashion in armor. So, in modern terms, the castle was
a sort of mixture of private residence, stronghold,
Town Hall, art gallery, and sports stadium, as well as
being a magistrates' court and county jail.

The whole of medieval society was controlled by
the lords, under the king, and the castles were the
seats of their power. All this, of course, puts everything too simply. Many lords had more than one
castle, and many castles were not owned by the lords
but by the king, while simple knights never actually
owned castles at all. The greater a lord was, the more

estates, towns, villages, castles, manors, and forests he owned. His whole scattered collection of landed property was called the *Honor*; the 'Honor of Warwick', for example, would mean the entire landed property — all over England and often with bits of France as well — of the Earls of Warwick. When a lord held many castles, each one would be looked after and lived in by a man of high rank in his own following who was called the *constable*. Thus many castles, and all the royal ones, had as well as their real owner a 'lord' whose permanent home it was, and often this 'lord', the constable, was a simple knight. He would keep the peace in the neighborhood or make wars in the interests of his overlords. While many castles were owned by the king, he didn't live in any of them permanently. But his lordship and control over them formed a great part of his power. In the many wars in England between the king and his barons, the success or failure of one side or the other depended a great deal on the control of the castles.

The constable of a castle made it his permanent home unless he was moved to another one, or lost his job, but a great lord who owned castles moved continually from one to the other, visiting in turn each part of his 'honor'. So did the kings, for they actually governed as well as ruled; they rode ceaselessly about their realms visiting every part of them, seldom staying for more than a few days in any one place. They took with them an army of officers and servants and an armed escort from the retinues of their household. There was always a group of the lords of the realm with them too, each with his own following, as well as the great officers of state with their own households and clerks.

The roads of Europe were full of movement, carrying this traffic of great households made up of men and women of all kinds and classes. The magnates travelled partly because they had to maintain personal control of their affairs, and partly because they needed to consume the food supplies of their estates. A great household, staying for five or six days on one manor or in one castle, would eat the place bare. If they stayed longer they would need to get supplies from farther afield, with awkward consequences. Most rents and dues were paid in kind — so many cattle or pigs, so much wheat, or so many fowl, eggs, fish, livestock, and produce of all kinds according to the district. These things could not be preserved or easily transported; they had to be eaten on the spot. So when the taxes and dues of a district were eaten up, the household moved on. This constant travelling made the lords familiar to their tenants and made the personal government of the monarchs real and effective, for his constant presence all over his realm made a medieval king very close to his subjects.

The very first castles were used mostly as forts; the latest ones mostly as residences. During the seven hundred or so years of the Age of Castles, their use as homes grew steadily while the need for them as forts declined. Even in the 12th century we find their domestic side emphasized. Here is a description, written in the first half of that century by one Lambert of Ardres, describing the timber tower, or keep, which in 1117 was built upon the earth mound: "Arnold, Lord of Ardres, built upon the motte of Ardres a wooden house, excelling all the houses of Flanders in that period both in material and in carpenter's work. The first storey was on the surface of the ground where were cellars, and granaries, and great boxes, tuns, casks, and other domestic utensils. In the storey above there were the dwellings and common living-rooms for the residents, in which were the larders, the rooms of the bakers and butlers, and the great chamber in which the Lord and his wife slept. Adjoining this was a private room, the dormitory of the waiting-maids and children. In the inner part of the great chamber was a certain private room, where at early dawn or in the evening or during sickness, or at times of blood-letting, or for warming the maids or weaned children, they used to have a fire. In the upper storey of the house were garret rooms in which on the one side the sons (when they wished it) and on the other side the daughters (because they were obliged) of the lord of the house used to sleep. In this storey also the watchmen and the servants appointed to keep the house took their sleep at some time or the other. High up on the east side of the house, in a convenient place, was the chapel which was made like unto the temple of Solomon by its gilding and painting. There were stairs and passages from storey to storey, from the home into the kitchen, from room to room and again from the house into the Loggia, where they used to sit in conversation or in recreation, and again from the Loggia into the Oratory."

At about the same time in England the historian

Manorbier Castle, the home of the historian Gerald de Barry (Giraldus Cambrensis), as it is today.

Gerald de Barry (Gerald of Wales, as he is generally called) was writing a description of his own family's castle at Manorbier in Pembrokeshire, which reads very much like a modern description of a gentleman's country house in a real estate agent's advertisement: "The castle called Maenor Pyrr is distant about three miles from Penbrock. It is excellently well defended by turrets and bulwarks and is situated on the summit of a hill extending on the Western side towards the seaport, having on the Northern and Southern sides a fine fish-pond under its walls, as conspicuous for its grand appearance as for the depths of its waters, and a beautiful orchard on the same side enclosed on one part by a vineyard and on the other by a wood, remarkable for the projection of its rocks and the height of its hazel trees. On the right hand of the promontory, between the castle and the church, near the site of a very large lake and mill, a rivulet of never-failing water flows through a valley, rendered sandy by the violence of the winds. Towards the west, the Severn sea, bending its course to Ireland, enters a hollow bay at some distance from the castle."

These descriptions were written by men of letters describing castles that they had seen, but after the middle of the 12th century written administrative records became common and many survive. From these we can learn how much care was given to the domestic parts of the castles, we can see what the living quarters were like, and we can get some idea of the life that went on within them. In the Public Record Office in Chancery Lane in London, there is a series of Rolls that list, among other things, the expenditure on the royal castles during the reign of Henry II, Richard I, John, Henry III, and Edward I, from 1154 to 1307. They go on beyond this, but we are mainly concerned with these 153 years. These records show how much was spent on the living quarters in the castles and exactly what improvements were made as time went on.

Medieval accounts were written on long sheets of parchment which had to be kept rolled up. The first set of these rolls, from 1184 to 1216, are called the 'Pipe Rolls', because they rolled up like pipes. The second kind, dating from 1216, are called the 'Liberate Rolls'. This name comes from the writs of 'liberate' set down upon them, that is, orders for the Exchequer to pay out (Latin *liberare*) certain sums of money, and the purpose for which they are to be paid.

The Pipe Rolls show, for instance, how Henry II built in stone a new royal lodging at Windsor, as well as a new stone wall with towers around the bailey. He built other residential buildings, too, inside the walls of the great round shell-keep on the mound and in the lower bailey. We read of the King's Hall and his rooms, larders, and kitchen, of the repairing of his and the queens's seats in the chapel, of pictures sent from London to the castle, and of a garden made within it. And we read how, at the same time, he made improvements at Winchester — a hall with hedges set about it — and had work done in the chapel and in the kitchens and upon a house for the King's falcons. Also there was painting done in the King's room, and a separate chapel to be prepared for the wife of his eldest son. At Nottingham, a castle that Henry II gave to his youngest and favorite son John, a new hall and private rooms were built between 1180 and 1183, and the keep was given a new timber floor. There was also a new almonry (a sort of estate office) and a mews for falcons, as well as gardens and a park. Henry II seems to have been fond of gardens, for he had one made outside his room at Arundel so that he could see it out of the window. King John seems to have been more interested in kitchens; at Marlborough and Ludgershall he made kitchens with ovens each big enough to roast two or three oxen at a time.

During the long reign of John's son, Henry III, a great deal was done to improve and enrich the living rooms in the royal castles. King Henry was a great connoisseur and patron of art — his rebuilding of Westminster Abbey is the greatest monument to his taste — and one of our most fastidious monarchs in the matter of personal comfort and luxury. His favorite castle was Winchester, where he had much fine work done. He built the beautiful hall, which still survives much as he left it, and later had all the cracks filled in, the paintwork redecorated, his chair on the dais repainted, and the paintings on the wall behind it renewed. In 1250 he ordered the Sheriff of Hampshire to have his new chapel painted and floored with tiles, to paint the table by his bed with "images of the guardians of Solomon's bed," to pave his room and the Queen's with tiles, to make wooden windows in the gallery of the Queen's chapel, and so on. He ordered tables and chairs and forms for his and the Queen's rooms, and had the Queen's room painted with green paint and supplied with new candlesticks and had a 'Majesty' painted with gilded images about it for her devotions. He also had a room between the kitchen and the great hall built for his stewards. (The stewards were officials responsible for the proper cooking and serving of meals.) There was also a new guard-room for his knights, a vaulted chamber which was to be wainscoted — that is, panelled all over in wood to keep out the coldness of the stone walls. This sort of wall-covering was still in general use up to the middle of the 19th century, and many panelled chambers can still be found today in houses great and small. Several of these rooms, dating from the 17th and 18th centuries, may be seen in the Victoria and Albert Museum in London and, apart from the actual design of the panelling, must look very much like Henry III's new guard-room at Winchester. This practice of wainscoting the stone walls of castle living-rooms seems to have become prevalent during the second half of the 13th century, for over and over again in the Liberate Rolls of Henry III we find reference to it. In 1239, after the birth of his eldest son (later Edward I) he orders the Bailiff of Windsor to "cause the chamber of our son Edward to be wainscoted, and iron bars to be made for the windows of the said chamber." We need not imagine such rooms as being dark; most panelled walls we see now are of old wood which has darkened with age. We find that medieval wainscot was generally painted. At Marlborough the Queen's room was "wainscoted and whitened," while one of the rooms at Windsor was to be "painted of a green colour with gold stars."

Glazed windows, too, were much in demand. At Marlborough, a new glazed window was put in the Queen's chapel, and in another of her rooms a window painted with a dove. At Windsor in 1236, when Henry married Eleanor of Provence, he had the Queen's Chambers redecorated for his bride;

glass was put into two of the windows overlooking the garden, "with shutters to open and shut," and another glass window in the gable was painted with the Tree of Jesse. Everywhere there was color; today, when we look at the mellow stone of an Abbey or a Cathedral, we may not realize that when it was new it blazed with color inside and out. Every piece of sculpture was brilliant in red and blue, green and yellow, while the gleam of gold-leaf shone from every surface. The West front of Wells Cathedral, built during Henry III's reign, with its numerous arches and columns and statues of saints and martyrs and kings, is splendid and beautiful now, because of the golden loveliness of the stone and the play of light and shadow over the sculpture and arcading. But what must it have looked like in 1250? Every bit of it was painted — the plain wall surfaces were white and every column, every capital, every arch as well as every statue was colored and gilded.

This passion for color was by no means confined to the churches, for the castles received the same treatment. Why, do you think, is the great keep of the castle in London called 'The White Tower'? It is grimly grey now, the only touch of white being the stonework at the corners; but in the Middle Ages it was whitewashed all over, partly to look good and partly to preserve the stone. Most castles were probably treated in the same way.

Inside, as we have seen, the walls were panelled and painted. At Windsor, Henry III had the cloister walls painted with pictures of the Apostles, under the eye of Mr. William of Westminster, the King's Painter, and at Hertford castle the walls of his 'Great Chamber' were whitened and diapered in colors. A century later, just after the frightful calamity that men called 'The Black Death', when one-third of England's population was wiped out in a few months, we find that the splendid and extravagant Edward III ordered the Sheriffs of the Southern counties to call up five hundred stone-masons and carpenters, glass-makers and jewellers to work in Windsor upon the castle and St. George's Chapel within it. He had them fitted with scarlet caps and liveries to prevent them from escaping and taking other jobs. This bright oufitting was done not only to make them conspicu-ous (so that they could be spotted and brought back if, in a time of acute labor shortage, they tried to get away to find better pay), but also to help to keep them satisfied and happy in their work. They got good wages, too. In 1349 many English painters, in the charge of Mr. Hugh of St. Albans, the King's Painter (a successor to Mr. William of Westminster, Painter to Henry III), began to cover the walls of St. Stephen's Chapel in the Palace of Westminster with a frieze of angels with peacock's wings and with pictures of Tobias, Job, and the Adoration of the Magi. These figures were shown in the court dress of the time, on a background of gilded gesso. All round the walls were arcades, or arched passage-ways, with statues of silver-gilt, leading up to a great golden figure of the Virgin and a picture by Hugh of

St. Albans of the King and his sons being presented before the throne of God by St. George.

In addition to lavish decoration, fireplaces too had become commonplace by the middle of the 13th century, not rarities as in the chamber in the 12th-century Ardres where "they used to have a fire." Henry III had fireplaces put into the living quarters of all the royal castles. Even so, cold must have been an ever-present problem. We read of the Lady Joan

One of the fireplaces in the 12th-century circular keep at Conisborough.

Berkeley, in Henry III's time, who "in her elder years used to saw up billets and sticks in her chamber, for which purposes she bought many fine handsaws." Certainly one way of keeping warm, though the picture of elderly ladies sawing up firewood is an unexpected one.

In a household of this kind there were always many boys of varying ages, being brought up among the

41

fighting men and the ladies. A boy generally went into training like this when he was only seven or eight years old. At first he would be what was called a page, learning to be useful about the domestic parts of the castle, particularly with the ladies, but he would very soon begin to learn the duties he would later have to perform as a Squire, in the stables and kennels, in the mews among his master's hawks, and in the armory. There was much to learn about the training and handling of horses, hounds, and hawks. In the armory he would learn not only how to care for armor and weapons, but how they were made, maintained, and repaired. This training would be not only theoretical, but practical as well. He would learn to ride, for instance, not just to be able to sit on a horse and get about on it, but to learn the complete art of managing a trained war-horse in the joust and in battle. He would learn the ways of all the different animals that had to be hunted — hunted for essential food, not just for sport. He would also learn the management of different kinds of weapons, and how to sustain the weight of warrior's armor. Even at the age of eight he would begin to wear armor; every castle's armory would contain many small harnesses for the boys in training, all of different sizes. (There are still a few of these small armors in existence, though most are later in date than the Middle Ages. There are however many swords of small size that have survived from as early as about 1250 — some suitable for a small boy of about seven, others a little bigger, for boys of ten or twelve. By the time a boy was thirteen or fourteen he would be quite strong enough to handle a full-sized weapon.) He would begin, then, to wear armor and wield weapons every day to get his muscles accustomed to the weight and to prepare his whole mind and body for the limitations it put upon his movement. Not that it was very heavy or particularly cramping; it wasn't. You can move about in armor nearly as freely as you can in ordinary clothes, but by learning to wear it and use it from such an early age, by the time he was fourteen and became a squire, a young man would find his armor as familiar to him as his own skin.

A page would learn a lot of other things too. He would be taught to dance, to sing, and to play upon various instruments — how to compose his own songs, too. Some boys probably weren't skilled at this, but many certainly were. He would learn how to carve every kind of bird and joint of meat, how to serve at table, how to handle wine properly, and how to look after the comfort of guests.

When a page became a squire, his duties about the castle and his training would be much the same only harder, with greater emphasis on the military side of it. If his lord took him on a campaign while he was still a page, he would not take part in the fighting, but would help to look after the comfort of his master and the knights who followed him on the march or in *billets*. In battle he would keep behind the fighting, with the baggage-train, tending the spare horses, ready to bring up a remount if his master was unhorsed. But when he became a squire he would fight at his lord's side, and guard him in the battle.

The squire served the knight, and the page served the squire. At no other period except the Middle Ages has service for its own sake been regarded as ennobling. In ancient times, service was for slaves. In modern times it is only done, rather reluctantly, for high wages. But during the Middle Ages it was regarded as a high honor for a boy to be allowed to serve at table, clean a guest's boots, or hold his stirrup while he mounted. As for carving the meat or pouring the wine, that was only for a senior squire or one of the household knights to do.

The actual training of pages and squires in these domestic and 'courteous' matters would be undertaken first by the ladies of the castle and by the chamberlain — a sort of glorified housekeeper — or in some special cases by the baron himself. But the essential fighting training seems to have been in the hands of an experienced, war-hardened man-at-arms, not necessarily a knight but usually a *sergeant*. This word was used to describe a professional cavalryman who fought in the same sort of armor as a knight, but was not of knightly rank, a man who in modern terms would be a trooper. Incidentally, you will find this word 'man-at-arms' (from the Latin *hominus ad armas*) very often in reading about medieval warfare. It was used to denote *all* men, knights and sergeants alike, who wore more-or-less complete armor and fought mounted — all heavy cavalrymen. This sergeant would see to the boys' training in the use of all kinds of weapons — sword, short spear, axe, mace, dagger, pole-axe, pole-hammer, and the cross-bow and the long bow — for a knight sometimes used these missile weapons as well as archers. He had to know how to use them, for he might be in command of a company of cross-bowmen or archers. A com-mander who can't use his own men's weapons isn't much use. The long lance, as distinct from the footman's spear, is only for use on horseback, and the use of this weapon could only be learned on a horse. Of course they used sword, axe, and mace on horseback as well as on foot, while the other weap-ons, having long shafts needing both hands, were for foot fighting. They would learn not only how to oppose sword with sword or axe with axe, but how to handle a sword against a man armed with a mace, or an axe against a man with a spear — opposing every kind of weapon with a different one. Experi-ence of unarmed combat, too, could be essential, as well as knowledge of woodcraft and all kinds of country lore. The squire would undergo all kinds of endurance tests, hardening him to exposure and the rigors of the weather. When he was not doing any of these things, he would spend a few minutes of the day swinging his sword or his axe to keep his muscles in trim. Somewhere in the castle bailey there would be one or two posts set up, about six feet high (about 2 meters), upon which the men-at-arms could prac-tice their strokes, cutting at them with sword and axe. There were probably also straw-filled sack dummies, for practicing spear work on, similar to those used by the Roman legionaries and by modern infantry-men for bayonet practice. There is a picture, too, in a 14th-century manuscript, showing a fully armed knight 'practising at the pell' as it was called.

Perhaps the most difficult of all the fighting arts was the management of the long lance on horseback. To be able to hit a small target, at a canter or a gallop, with a nine-foot spear tucked under your arm, is no easy matter. Not only do you have to aim your point at your target, you have to aim your horse at it too so that he brings you into the correct place and position for you to be able to hit it. (I have described something about lance-practice in another book, *A Knight and His Horse*, so I won't go into it again here).

In the chronicles of Jean Froissart, a contemporary of Chaucer, we find some interesting references to the part squires played in battle. For instance, in his account of the battle of Poitiers, fought on September 19, 1356, there are several passages describing how knight's squires fought beside him, how they looked after him after the battle was over, and how they came to wealth and position because of it. He tells us how Sir James Audley, one of the Black Prince's household knights, came up to him when the French began to advance upon the English position. He asked if he might have permission to fight in the forefront of the battle, instead of staying with the reserve near the Prince's person with his staff. "Sir," he said. "Some time ago I made a vow that if I was ever engaged in a battle where the King your father or any of his sons were, I should be foremost

46

A Norman 'chevalier' of the late 11th century.
These are the men the Saxons called 'cnihtas'.

in the attack, and the best fighter on his side, or die in the attempt. I beg therefore, most earnestly, that you will give me permission to leave your company with honor so that I can put myself in a position where I can accomplish my vow." So Sir James set off and posted himself in the front of the line, with four squires whom he had kept with him to guard his person.

Later, Froissart mentions Sir James again. "The Lord James Audley, attended by his four squires, was always engaged in the heart of the battle. He was severely wounded, but as long as his strength and breath permitted he maintained the fight and continued to advance. At last, when he was quite exhausted, his four squires led him to a hedge so that he could cool himself and get his breath back. They disarmed him as gently as they could, so that they could look at his wounds, dress them, and sew up the most dangerous."

When the battle was over, and the Prince was settled in his tent in Maupertuis village, he asked his knights if they had heard anything of Sir James Audley. They told him that he was wounded and lying on a stretcher. The Prince asked if he was well enough to be brought to him. "If not," he said, "I will go to him myself." Two of the knights went to Sir James, and he got some men to lift him and carry him on his stretcher to the Prince's tent. They laid him down, and the Prince bent down and embraced him, saying, "My lord, I have to honor you very much, for by your valor this day you have gained honor and glory above us all, and your prowess has proved you the bravest knight. And to increase your renown, and to provide for you so that you can continue your career of glory in war, I retain you from now on as my knight, with a yearly revenue of 500 marks, which I will secure to you from my estates in England." "Sir," said Lord James, "God make me deserving of the good fortune you bestow upon me."

But he did a very fine thing with that 500 marks a year. When he'd been carried back to a tent that had been pitched for him, he asked four knights, who were close relatives to him, to come to him. He told them of the Prince's gift, and then said, "You see here these four squires, who have always served me most nobly, and especially so in today's battle. Whatever glory I may have gained has been because of them, and by their valor. I want to reward them; so in the same way as I have received the Prince's gift, I disinherit myself of it, and give it to them."

Most people think of medieval knights in the same way as they think of 'cowboys', those heroes of the old days in the American West. These men are always presented in Westerns as young and fearless, handsome righters of wrongs and rescuers of distressed folk. We see them constantly shooting outlaws and riding about very splendidly, but they never appear to do any work, though of course we know quite well that real cowboys worked very hard. So it is with knights.

Let us see what they really wore, what they had to do, and how they got their living.

At first they weren't called *knights* at all. They were just soldiers trained to fight on horseback in armor — mail and leather armor, not plate-armor. They were called simply, horsemen. In France they were *chevaliers*, *caballeros* in Spain, *cavalliere* in Italy, and *equites* in Latin. In Germany they were called *Reiters* — riders — which means the same thing. So why do we call them *knights*? It is an Anglo-Saxon word, and to find out how these horsemen got this name in England we must go back to the times before the Norman conquest in 1066, to the times when Europe was being attacked and raided on all sides by hordes of fierce fighting men. From the North came the Vikings, from the East, raiding what is now Hungary and Austria, came savage tribes called Magyars, while up from the South the victorious Muslim Arabs or Saracens drove through Spain and threatened France. The rulers of the peoples of western Europe had to try to stop these raids and invasions from becoming an occupation. The only way to do this was to raise forces of fighting men, well armed and trained to fight in the most effective way possible. And during this period the best way was on horse-back, armed with lance and sword and protected by helmet, shield, and mail shirt. It had been found that such warriors, acting together in troops, were able to beat Vikings, Magyars, and Saracens. So every ruler had to set about getting as many of these chevaliers as he could. He did this through his bar-ons; he gave them land to hold in return for service to him. To perform this service, each baron had to build a castle and bring a certain number of fighting men to the royal army whenever he was called upon, so many chevaliers and so many foot soldiers, accord-ing to the size of the land he held. Every baron had to be responsible for bringing in these soldiers. He retained them by giving them, in turn, pieces of his land which they paid for with service to him, and through him to the King. The piece of land held in this way was called a *fee*, or *fief,* and the whole of this system of service in return for land was called *Feudal.*

It began on the European Continent. In England, the Saxon Kings dealt with Viking raids and invasions in a different way. When a raiding force landed, everyone between the ages of sixteen and sixty was expected to turn out to fight; but they fought on foot, using the same arms and tactics as their enemies. There were no chevaliers. So when Duke William of Normandy landed in 1066 with all of his feudal warriors, the two different types of fighting forces met. As we know, the old Saxon method was no match for the mounted chivalry of the continental army.

After the conquest, King William had to reward his followers. He had no large sums of money, nor would his barons have wanted that even if he had. It was land they were after, and land — English land, the property of dead or defeated Saxon lords — was what William gave them. On this land these barons built castles, strongholds from which they held down the conquered English. The leaders of his army and the lesser captains under them were given lands to hold for the King. But they had to pay for them by promising to serve the King, each with his own following of fighting men. To the dispossessed and beaten English, these chevaliers in the service of their lords seemed to be just what they were — young soldiers in service. So they used the Anglo-Saxon word for such men — *cnihtas,* or knights.

51

*A knight of the mid-15th century, wearing a
full harness of plate.*

So in England a knight was just a mounted soldier.
And a hard-bitten, hard-riding, hard-drinking, foul-
mouthed fellow he was, of the toughest, roughest
kind. What happened then, to turn such a ruffian of
the 11th century into the courteous gentleman of the
14th? Well, once the terrible raiding and savaging of
the Vikings and Magyars and Saracens was held and
beaten back, the people who lived in England,
France, Germany, Spain, and Italy — what we might
call the whole of European society — could settle
down. They wanted a gentler and more civilized way
of living. They were hindered though, by their own
frightful warriors, the very fighting men they had
produced to protect themselves. Now that they
didn't need the protection, the chevaliers or knights
had no work to do. So of course they fought each

other, and it was left to the Church to try to find an answer to the problem. One thing the Church tried to do was to decree what was called 'The Truce of God', which laid down that nobody was to fight between Thursday night and Tuesday morning — a sort of long week-end off — on pain of excommunication. Naturally enough this didn't work. Then, right at the end of the 11th century, the Church was given a splendid opportunity. In 1171, the Saracens, not Arabs but a much fiercer people called Turks, beat the great army of the Emperor of Constantinople and overran all of Asia Minor, and Palestine, and Syria as well. This was a very serious matter, and it will perhaps be worthwhile going into it in more detail. A large part of Eastern Europe (what is now Rumania, Bulgaria, and Greece) as well as much of Asia (those parts around the Black Sea, with 'Asia Minor', now Turkey) and part of Northern Syria, was still 'The Roman Empire'. In 364 the old Empire of Rome was divided into two parts, the Western Empire of Italy, Spain, Gaul, and Britain, ruled from Rome, and the Eastern Empire ruled from Byzantium and Constantinople (now called Istanbul). When the old Roman Empire fell to pieces in the West, the Eastern half survived. It was this great, wealthy, populous Empire that, after 1171, was threatened by the Turkish Saracens.

Palestine, of course, mattered very much because Christ himself had lived and taught there. Christians from all over Europe went on long and difficult journeys — pilgrimages — to places like Nazareth and

53

Jerusalem, and regarded the whole country as holy.
We still call it the Holy Land. When it was overrun
by these savage Turks, it was very serious. The Arabs,
who had occupied it before 1171, didn't mind Christians and allowed them to come and go as they liked,
visiting the Holy Places. But the Turks, Muslims like
the Arabs, hated Christianity. They closed the Holy
Places, massacred pilgrims, and forced Christians to
become Muslims or else die.

The Emperor at Constantinople appealed to the
Pope in Rome for help. The Pope appealed to Chris-
tendom — that is, to all the people living in Christian
Europe. He called on the men to stop fighting each
other and to go eastwards and fight the Turks instead. This appeal, and the news of the terrible
happenings in Asia, fired the imagination of every-
body who heard it; so much so that from all parts of
France and Germany masses of people, ordinary
working folk as well as knights and fighting men, set
off on the long journey to the Holy Land.

Of course, they didn't all go. But this Crusade
marked a turning point, for so many unemployed
warriors went off that the more responsible people
who stayed at home were better able to organize
their affairs and the life of their communities. And
at about the same time, the land-holding classes in
France invented for themselves another idea, which
had a great effect in turning the tough bully of a
Cniht into Chaucer's "verray parfit, gentil Knight."
They called it 'the Gay Science', what we know as
Chivalry. This set out a code of decent behavior,

among other things that every boy of a warrior family should take an oath when he was twelve, before a Bishop, that he "would defend to the uttermost the oppressed, the widow and the orphan, and that women, particularly those of noble birth, should enjoy his especial care." He also had to promise to defend the Church and always to be ready to fight in its cause. Furthermore, he was expected to be cheerful, always; to speak quietly and not to show off; to think and talk sense, or not talk at all; to be gracious and well-mannered — all those social graces that make a person nice to be with. All this he had to promise when he was twelve. He had, of course, to be a good fighter as well. Not just a good natural fighter, but a hard professional soldier trained to fight on his own or in company with other knights. He had to keep himself very fit and be able to do things that today may seem to be beyond the strength of any man. He had to be brave, too. Part of his code was to fear nothing and nobody, ever. And he had to be loyal, particularly to his own lord, to his monarch, and to the Christian Church.

So much for his code of knightly behavior. What about his job? As in the time of William the Conqueror, he had to serve his lord as a soldier — not only in war, but also in peacetime for part of every year on garrison-duty in one of his lord's castles, and also for a time as a member of his lord's escort in his constant journeyings. And of course he had to look after his own fee, his land, tenants, and servants. He often had to sit in his Manor Court among the people living on his land and settle their quarrels and sit in judgment on their crimes. When he grew in age and experience he had to sit as a magistrate in the Shire Court. He was a bit like a policeman, too, but really much more like a deputy in the old West. He had to see that law and order were maintained, and if the sheriff called out the *posse comitatus* he had to get into his armor and join his brother knights in his shire to hunt down criminals and outlaws. It was often a hard and dangerous duty. In England, though there were many civil wars, rebellious and national disturbances all through the Middle Ages, as well as a good deal of private warring between rival barons, a knight's duty was most often of a police kind.

Such, briefly, is what a knight was, and what he had to do. But suppose he had no land, no fee to hold, no 'knight service' owed to a lord? There were many knights like this. The best thing that they could do was to become simply professional soldiers and enter the service of some wealthier knight or baron as a retainer, getting their keep in return for their service. Whatever else they needed they had to win for themselves by their own ability. The main aim of any landless knight was, somehow, to get a fee or fief for himself. Some achieved this by outstanding service, others by a fortunate love affair leading to marriage with an heiress. Independent souls would not bind themselves permanently to any lord, but would wander all over Europe seeking adventure and advancement wherever it was to be found. Knights who did this were called *knights errant*, or wandering knights.

Actually, it was possible to make a good living, even to gain great wealth and influence, by going about the world fighting in tournaments. To achieve this all you needed was to be a good fighter, an entertaining person, and a good companion, open-handed and generous. By the rules of war and of its image, the tournament, if you were able to overcome another knight in fair fight and capture his person, you gained his horse and arms and could get from him a ransom according to his means. If you were lucky enough to capture a great lord you might make your fortune in an afternoon. Of course it was a risky business, for you were just as likely to lose all you possessed. Then, until you could find a friend or a patron to stand the expense of re-equipping you, you were in no position to fight at all. This was why you needed to be more than just a good fighter; if you could sing nicely, or play, and were the sort of person whose company others enjoyed, sooner or later you would find someone to help you. This was, more often than not, a lady. It was one of the graces of medieval society that the love of fair ladies was a good thing, and as important to a knight's advancement as military success.

Castle Buildings

Man has always needed to defend himself and his property from the rapacity of his neighbors, and the art of fortification is very old. Everywhere you go, all over Europe and Asia, you can find traces of fortresses, some very ancient, some more recent, and many entirely modern. The castle may appear to be only one among these, but in fact it is quite different from any kind of fortification that came before or after it. The great hill-forts of the Iron Age Celts, the *duns* of Ireland and Scotland, and the Roman *camps* were fortifications in which whole tribes or armies could take shelter with all their goods and cattle in times of war. The *burhs* of Saxon England and of the Teutonic lands of Europe were for the same purpose. Ethelfreda, daughter of Alfred the Great, built the burh of Worcester "to shelter all the folk." Our modern word borough comes, of course, from this Anglo-Saxon word (Pittsburg, Williamsburg, Edinburgh), just as 'chester' (in Rochester, Manchester, Lancaster) comes from the Latin word 'caster'. These were in no sense castles; a castle was the private fortress and dwelling place of a lord and his family. In European society during the late Middle Ages, from about A.D. 1000 to A.D. 1500, a period which might just as properly been called The Age of Castles as The Age of Chivalry, these lords were the rulers of the land. 'Lord', of course, is the word used in England only. It comes from the Anglo-Saxon word *hlaford*. *Hlaf* was a loaf, and *hlaford* was a loaf-giver, which suggests a kind, paternal protector, not an iron-fisted soldier. In France, the Lord was called *Seigneur;* in Spain, *Señor;* in Italy, *Signor,* all derived from the Latin *senior,* meaning, literally *elder.* In Germany and the Teutonic lands it was *Herr* or *Heer* or *Her.*

The English language always produced words of its own, as we saw with the word *knight.* This *loaf-giver* meaning of the word was in fact largely true in Anglo-Saxon times; and it must have been difficult and bitter to the conquered English to have to apply this name to the new, all-powerful Norman seigneurs who ruled the country after 1066. It was these *lords* who built the first great castles in England, and until the 14th century they and their knightly retainers spoke in Norman-French. Until the 13th century they thought of themselves as French, too; most of them held lands and castles in Normandy and Brittany, and their names were the names of French towns and villages—Baliol, from Bailleul, Sacheverell, from Saute de Chevreuil, for instance, and Beauchamp, Beaumont, Bures, Lacy, Clare, and so on.

The castles we are now so familiar with are not much like the castles built by these Norman barons in their own country or in England, for these were generally constructed in timber, and not of stone. There are a very few early stone castles (the great keep of the Tower of London is one still surviving almost unaltered) which were built at the end of the 11th century, but the great age of castle-building in stone did not begin until about 1150. The early castles relied for their defenses mainly upon the age-old principle of the earth work, and were similar to the ones that had been raised on the continent for the previous 200 years. The first castles were built in the Frankish Kingdom as a defense against the violence of the Vikings. A castle of this kind consisted of an oblong or circular earth work — a ditch and earth bank enclosing a comparatively small area — with a great mound of earth either at one end or in the middle. The bank was crowned with a stockade of timber, as was the top of the mound. Inside the stockade was a timber keep. Except for the mound, the whole structure was very like those timber blockhouses built by the pioneers in the early days of the American West.

This type of castle is called the *motte and bailey* castle. The motte was the great mound that formed the central citadel — a word that later changed to *moat* and meant something quite different, the ditch encircling the whole castle. The bailey was the area enclosed by the outer bank and stockade. The timber keep built upon the motte was usually raised on four great corner posts, clear of the ground. There is a description of one of these castles in a biography of Bishop John of Terouenne, written in about 1130: "Bishop John used to stay frequently at Merchem when he was going round his diocese. Near the churchyard was an exceedingly high fortification, which might be called a Castle, built according to the fashion of the country by the lord of the Manor many years before. For it is the custom of the nobles of that region who spend their time for the most part in private war, in order to defend themselves from the attacks of their enemies, to make a hill of earth as high as they can and encircle it with a ditch as broad and deep as possible. They surround the upper edge of the hill with a very strong wall of hewn logs, placing small towers on its circuit, according to their means. Inside this wall they put their home or keep which overlooks the whole thing. The entrance to this fortress is only by a bridge that rises from the counterscarp of the ditch, supported by double or even triple columns until it reaches the upper edge of the hill." The biographer goes on to say how one day, as the Bishop and his attendants were crossing this bridge, it collapsed and threw them thirty-five feet (about 11 meters) into the ditch below.

The motte was generally from thirty to forty feet high (9 to 12 meters), though there is an exceptional one in Norfolk, at Thetford, which is a hundred feet high (about 30 meters). It was flat on top and the upper palisade enclosed an area of about fifty or sixty yards square. The bailey varied in extent from about one and a half acres to about three acres (less than 2 hectares) — rarely very large. The shape varied —some were oblong, some square, some shaped like a figure eight. There were endless possibilities of variation dictated by the wealth of the builder or the configuration of the ground. Once the site had been chosen, the first thing to do was to dig out the ditch around it; the earth dug out was thrown on to the inside of the ditch to form the bank or *scarp*. The outer rim of the ditch was called the *counterscarp*. If it was possible, the ditch was dug around a natural mound, but often this had to be raised by an immense amount of spadework.

Reconstruction of an 11th-century 'motte and bailey' castle. The bailey, here a separate enclosure, is surrounded by a stout palisade of timber, with a ditch all around the outside. The motte, or mound, has its own ditch, and a high palisade crowns the top, surrounding the timber tower. It is reached from the bailey by a long flying bridge, defended at its lower end by two small square towers. The upper section would have been in the form of a drawbridge. If an attacking force captured the bailey, the defenders would retire up the bridge into the stockade on the top of the mound. The drawbridge would have been of very light construction and they would probably have thrown the whole thing down behind them.

Such were the castles built all over England after the conquest in 1066. We even have a nearly contem-

porary picture of one of them being built in the
Bayeux Tapestry, where Duke William's men — or
more probably rounded-up Saxon laborers — are
shown building the motte of the castle of Hastings.
The Anglo-Saxon Chronicle tells, under the year
1067, how the Normans "wrought Castles widely
throughout the Nation, and oppressed the poor
people." In the Domesday Book is the record of the
houses that had to be demolished in order to build
castles — 116 demolished at Lincoln, for instance,
and 113 at Norwich. This sort of easily built fortress
was exactly what the Normans needed to follow up
their victory at Hastings and to hold down the hostile
English, for they could go up very quickly. It is
interesting to find that, a century later, when the
Anglo-Normans under Henry II were trying to con-
quer the Irish, they built precisely the same kind of
motte-and-bailey castles in Ireland, although in
England and on the continent great castles of stone
had by this time replaced the old earthwork-and–
palisade ones.

A few of these stone castles were new, on fresh
sites, but most of them were rebuilds of the old ones.
Sometimes the keep would be rebuilt in stone while
the old stockade still defended the bailey, while in
other cases a new wall of stone was built round the
bailey, leaving the old timber keep on the motte. At
York, for instance, the old timber tower stood upon
the motte for nearly 200 years, long after a stone wall
had been built around the bailey, until Henry III
replaced it with the great keep, which still exists,

between 1245 and 1272. A few of the new stone keeps were built upon the old mottes, though this was usually only when the mound itself was a natural one; the great weight of a stone keep would be insecure if it were to have been placed on top of a mound of earth only dug about a century before. In some cases, where the artificial mound had not settled enough, the keep was actually built round it, incorporating the old mound in its own base, as at Kenilworth. In other cases, instead of a tower keep the old palisade on top of a motte would be replaced by a high stone wall enclosing the whole area of the mound's top. Inside this wall all the living quarters, storerooms, etc. were built. Such buildings are today called *shell keeps* — the Round Tower at Windsor is an example, and good ones survive at Restormel, Tamworth, Cardiff, Arundel, and Carisbrooke. The walls of the bailey were carried up the sides of the mound, as the old palisades had been, to join the walls of the shell on either side.

The *tower keep* is more common in England. In the Middle Ages this was more often called the *donjon* or simply the *tower*. The first word has changed its meaning, for no one today thinks of a castle keep when they speak of a dungeon; it has come to mean the nastier kind of prison. And, of course, the reason why the castle in London is called 'The Tower' is because it has retained its original name.

The keep formed the central strong point or citadel of the castle. On the ground floor would be storerooms for most of the food and arms in the

Pembroke Castle, showing the great cylindrical 'donjon' built in 1200 by William Marshall.

castle; above it were the guard-rooms, kitchens, and living quarters for the garrison, while on the upper floors lived the lord of the castle and his family and retainers. The military role of the keep was purely defensive, for here within its unscalable and immensely strong walls even a tiny garrison could hold out as long as supplies lasted. As we shall see, there were times when the keep of a castle was stormed, or so damaged that it became untenable, but these were rare; most keeps fell either because of treachery or starvation. The problem of water was seldom serious, for there was always a well inside a keep— you can still see the one in the Tower of London.

The shell-keep was quite common, perhaps because it was the easiest thing to add to an existing
motte-and-bailey castle, but the feature that is absolutely typical of the medieval castle, particularly in
England, is the great rectangular tower. The object
of its design was that it should be impregnable. To
this end it was the most massive construction. The
walls were tremendously thick, splayed out at the
base to defy the picks, bores, and rams of the besiegers, and rising sheer to the battlements seventy or
eighty feet above (20 to 25 meters). Flat buttresses
called pilasters strengthened the sides and corners,
at each angle rising to a turret over-topping the roof.
The entrance was always well above ground level on
the first floor, reached by an outside staircase set at
right angles to the door and covered by a rectangular
tower-like forebuilding set against the face of the
wall. For obvious reasons the windows were very
small. There were none on the ground floor, very
small ones on the first floor and only slightly larger
ones on the upper level. These features, the outside
staircase, forebuildings and windows, can be seen
very well at Rochester and at Castle Hedingham in
Essex.

The walls were built of rag-stone or rubble encased
with outer and inner faces of ashlar, a more smoothly
finished stone, except in a few very early examples
like the White Tower in London. At Dover, built by
Henry II in 1170, the walls of the keep are from
twenty-one feet to twenty-four feet thick (about 6 to
7 meters); at Rochester they are twelve feet thick (3.7

The keep of Rochester Castle, Kent. Built by Henry II in 1165, it was besieged by King John in 1214 and overrun when his miners brought down the northwest angle turret. The present cylindrical turret was built to replace the fallen one in 1200 by Henry III. The forebuilding can be seen on the right of the picture.

meters) at the base tapering to ten feet (3 meters) at the top. The upper and safer parts of the wall were generally a little less thick, being reduced on the inside at each floor level, thereby gaining a little in space and saving a little in weight and in stone. In the larger towers, such as London, Colchester, Rochester, Hedingham, and Dover, the inside was divided in two by a stout cross-wall up the middle from top to bottom, the upper parts of which were lightened by being pierced with arches. This can still be seen clearly in the Tower of London. These cross-walls added strength to the structure and made it easier to floor and roof the building, as without the wall the spans would be too great. A cross-wall could have direct military advantages too. At Rochester in 1215, when King John besieged the castle, his miners succeeded in bringing down the north-west corner turret of the keep. The besieging force broke in, but the defenders got behind the cross-wall and held their half of the keep for some time longer.

The larger and taller tower keeps were divided into a basement and three upper floors, the smaller into a basement and two floors, though there are of course exceptions — Corfe, a very tall keep, had only two upper floors, so had Guildford, while Norham had four. Some, like Kenilworth, Castle Rising, and Middleham, which were oblong in plan and not very tall, had only a basement and one main upper floor.

Each floor was devised as one large room, divided into two if there was a cross-wall. The basement was used for storage: provisions for the garrison and their horses and for its many servants, arms of all kinds, and all the stores necessary for the upkeep of a castle in peace and war — stone and timber for repairs, paint, tallow, hides, ropes, bales of cloth and canvas, and probably a good deal of quicklime and combustible oil to pour over besiegers. Often the very top floor would have been divided by wooden partitions into small rooms, and in a few cases like Dover and Hedingham the main room — the hall on the second floor — occupied two whole stories which gave a lofty hall with wall-galleries round it. (The keep at Norwich, now used as a museum, is arranged in this way and gives an idea of how it would have looked.) In the more important keeps there were fireplaces in the upper stories, and many good early

The keep of Castle Hedingham, Essex, built in 1100. The steps leading to the doorway can be seen on the left of the picture; originally, a forebuilding as at Rochester covered its entrance.

examples survive. Where there was no fireplace, the chamber was probably heated by a large iron brazier.

The staircases giving access to the different floors were built specially in the angles of the keep and were continued up into the turrets so that the roof could be reached. These staircases spiralled upwards in a clockwise direction. This was deliberate, for if any defender had to fight on the stairs because an enemy had broken into the keep at ground level, they would have a double advantage: they would be trying to push their assailants down the stairs, and they would have their left sides, where they carried their shields, against the central pillar of the stair, while on their right would be plenty of space, even in a narrow stairway, to swing their weapons. The attackers would have to fight their way up, their weapons hampered by the central pillar. Try this the next time you are on a spiral stairway and you will see what I mean.

The Great Hall in the keep of Hedingham Castle in Essex. The arch spanning it from the left to right in the picture is the upper part of the cross-wall which divided the keep into two sections. Solid in the lower floors, it was built as an arch in the upper floor to lighten the weight and give more space in the hall.

In the upper levels of a keep many small chambers were hollowed out in the thickness of the walls to make private rooms where the lord of the castle and his family and guests might sleep; in the same way the latrines were built into the thickness of the walls.

These were skillfully designed; medieval sanitation was better than we like to think. The lavatories in a medieval castle were very much more satisfactory and easier to keep clean than the old-fashioned earth-closets that can still be found in use in country places. They were small chambers built out to overhang the wall, open underneath. The necessary seats were built of wood over these openings, and everything went straight out into the air. They used to call the latrine the *garderobe*, a polite word for it, meaning literally 'guard your robe'. In the same way the Elizabethans called their lavatories 'the jakes', and in America we politely refer to 'the john', in England, 'the loo'.

A well was of course an absolutely essential feature in a castle keep. Sometimes, as in the Tower of London, this came up in the basement, but in many keeps it was carried right up into the residential floors, which was safer and more convenient. Another thing that was considered essential was a chapel, in case the garrison was cut off in the keep after the bailey, where the main chapel was, had fallen. The beautiful chapel in the White Tower in London is the finest surviving example of a chapel built within a keep; its more usual place was in the forebuilding, a small and simple chamber over the doorway.

Late in the 12th century some important changes began to take place in the design of the tower keeps. The rectangular tower, massively strong though it was, had one weakness — its sharp angles. The stone in these corners could be picked and battered away, while the attackers who worked at them were almost invisible, and quite unreachable, except from the turret immediately above. To do away with this risk and disadvantage to the defense, many keeps were built on a circular plan, and great cylindrical towers like the keep at Pembroke built in 1200 by William Marshal began to rise. Some were of a transitional kind, a sort of compromise between the old rectangular design and the new cylindrical one; these had many sides and no sharp angles. Examples are the keeps at Orford in Suffolk and Conisborough in Yorkshire, the former built by Henry II between 1165 and 1173, the latter by his half-brother Earl Hamelin de Warenne during the 1190s.

The stone walls that replaced the old stockades round the baileys were built on the same military principles as the keeps. They were as high and as thick as possible; the lower part was generally splayed out, to give strength to the most vulnerable part and to provide a sloping surface from which stones and other missiles dropped from above would splinter and ricochet out among the attackers at the foot of the wall. The top was crenellated — that is, finished with what we today call *battlements*. This crenellation was devised like this: along the top of the wall was a fairly broad walk or platform, called *alatorium* in Latin, from which it derived its technical name of *allure*. On the outside this was protected by another wall, a parapet about seven to eight feet high (about 2.5 meters), broken by openings at regular intervals.

A reconstruction of a flanking tower and the walls of the 13th-century bailey. The tower is cylindrical on the outside, facing the field, but flat on the inner side. There is a small crane on the wall at the back of the tower for hoisting up ammunition to the defenders working in the hoarding. The high roof is built of stout timbers covered with tiles or stone shingles, or slates. The top of the tower below the roof has its timber hoardings in position. You can see how an attacker, having crossed the moat, would be exposed to the shot of archers in the tower as well as from the hoardings above. The rampart walk is shown, on the walls, as well as some of the lean-to buildings against the inside of the wall.

These openings are called *embrasures* and the pieces of parapet between them are called *merlons*. The openings allowed the defenders to shoot down or drop things upon their assailants, but they had to expose themselves to do so before dodging back into the cover provided by the merlons. For this reason the merlons themselves were often provided with arrow-slits through which the defenders could shoot from cover. These arrow-slits were long, very narrow openings set vertically in the wall or merlon, only about two or three inches wide (about 5 to 8 centimeters) at the outside but opening out inside to give room for a bowman to use his weapon. They were about six feet deep (about 2 meters), with a short cross-slit set a little above half-way up to allow the archers to shoot sideways at an angle of about forty-five degrees. There were many variations in the actual shapes of these slits, but the principle was always the same. You can imagine how difficult it would have been for an attacking archer or crossbowman to shoot an arrow or a bolt through one of these slits, but if you visit a castle and stand on the inside of an arrow-slit you will see how well you can see the "field" below your wall and how much room there is in the arrow-slit for you to handle your bow or crossbow.

Of course, a perfectly plain wall encircling the bailey would have many disadvantages, for once the attackers reached the foot of it you couldn't really get at them. If you leaned right out of the embrasures you would be shot; if you kept under the cover of the merlons you couldn't see the foot of the wall to shoot down to it. So it was better to break the wall at intervals with towers or *bastions* which projected forward into the field, and from arrow-slits in their

Various kinds of arrow-slits. In many castles there are different sorts of arrow-slits in different parts of the castle. Most had short transverse slits to allow a bowman to shoot a little sideways, but many were made without these. They were generally between 4 feet and 7 feet long.

sides or from their battlements you could shoot sideways along the wall, thus *enfilading* (as it was called) your enemy at the foot of it. These towers were at first rectangular, but later made in the form of half-cylinders set against the wall, the inside of each bastion flush with the flat inner face of the bailey wall. They were carried up to over-top the wall, thus breaking up the parapet walk into sections. The walk passed through each bastion, but these passages were closed by stout doors. So if an assault party got up to the top of a part of the wall, it could be cut off between two towers and destroyed.

The castles visible in England today are usually unroofed and flat on top, except for the battlements, but when they were in use the towers and bastions were often capped by steep roofs, as one may so

Diagram showing the way that the hoardings, or 'brattices', were added to the bailey walls. These were probably only put up when the castle was likely to be besieged. In many castle walls you can still see the square holes, just below the battlements, where the great horizontal beams which held up the hoardings were put.

often see on the European Continent. We tend to forget, when we look at a ruined castle like Usk, Dover, or Conisborough, what a great deal of perishable woodwork and roofing there would have been. Often the tops — the parapet walks — of bailey walls, towers, and even keeps were capped with long wooden galleries, roofed over, called *hoardings* (Latin *hurdicia*), or *brattices*. These galleries were built out to project about six feet (about 2 meters) forward over the outer face of the wall; openings were made in the floor of this projecting part through which sundry things like quicklime, lumps of rock, boiling fat, boiling water, and arrows could be sent down to the attacking force. The disadvantages of these timber hoardings were that they could easily be broken down by the stones hurled from the besiegers' 'engines', and were easily burnt.

The most vulnerable part of a bailey wall was its gate, and right from the beginning this was given extra defenses. The earliest of these were in the form of strong, square towers containing the gate; a good example is the 11th-century gate at Exeter which still survives. During the 13th century most of these square gatehouses were converted into keeps by blocking up the gates and adding extra stories, as at Richmond and Ludlow. In the 12th century a more usual way of defending the gate was to build a large tower on either side of the gateway, and in the 13th the gatehouse proper appears. The twin flanking towers are now joined solidly together above the gate, and the whole thing becomes a strong and massive unit and one of the most important features in the whole castle. The gateway itself has become quite a long and narrow entrance passage, blocked at either end by a *portcullis*. This is a gate that slides vertically up and down in grooves cut in the stone work at each side. It was made in the form of a great grid or grille of heavy timber, the bottom ends of the vertical members being cut into points and shod with iron; thus, the bottom edge of the portcullis is a row of great iron spikes. The portcullis was moved by thick ropes working on a winch which was housed in the chamber above the entrance passage; in the 'Bloody Tower' in the Tower of London you can see the portcullis and its machinery. The entrance passage was further defended by *meurtrieres*, or 'murder-holes' pierced in the vault above, through which the defender could drop the usual things upon anyone who tried to force the gates. However, it is likely that the primary purpose of these holes was to enable the defenders to pour down water to quench fires in the passage, for by far the best way to force an entry was to stuff the passage full of straw, brushwood and so on, preferably well soaked in fat, set fire to it, burn the portcullis, and roast the defenders in the chambers above. Along each side of many entrance passages were narrow chambers built in the wall, with small horizontal arrow-slits giving on to the passage, through which a few crossbowmen could shoot at horribly close range into the packed mass of assailants in the passage as they tried to break in.

In the upper parts of these gatehouses were guardrooms and often residential apartments, and in special chambers in the towers were the winches that worked the great chains for raising and lowering the drawbridge.

Because the gate was the place where an assault was most often made, it often had extra defenses, called the *barbican*, built out in front of it. This usually consisted of two long, high walls running

A reconstruction of the gatehouse and barbican of the Castle at Arques in France. The barbican is an elaborate outwork covering the main gatehouse, with two drawbridges.

parallel forward from the gate, thus forcing an attack to approach the gate through a narrow passage, exposed all the while to the shot of archers on the gatehouse and on the battlemented walls of the barbican. Sometimes, to make the approach even more hazardous, the passage was set at an angle to the gate, forcing the attackers to come from the right of the gate so that the unshielded right sides were exposed to the arrows of the defenders. The end of the barbican passage was usually covered by some sort of outwork, often quite elaborate. At Goodrich in Herefordshire, for instance, it takes the form of a large semi-circular covering wall, while the two barbicans covering the gates at Conway are like small outer baileys.

The gatehouse at Warwick, built in the middle of the 14th century by Thomas Beauchamp, Earl of Warwick (Earl Richard's grandfather), is a good example of a compact gatehouse and barbican, built as one splendidly designed unit. The gatehouse itself is built on the traditional plan of two flanking towers joined above a narrow entrance passage. The gatehouse has three upper stories, and tall battlemented turrets rise at each corner above the battlements of the roof. In front, two battlement walls enclose another narrow passage leading to the gate; at the far end of these barbican walls, facing the field, is another pair of towers like a smaller gatehouse. In front of this was the drawbridge over the moat. So an attacker trying to force the gate would first have to cross the moat, then burn or batter his way through the raised drawbridge covering the first gate and portcullis behind it. Then he would have to fight his way along the narrow passage of the barbican. Then, in front of the gate proper, there was a second gap to cross and another raised drawbridge and portcullis to force. When he got through this he would be in the narrow passage exposed to the meurtrieres and the arrow-slits in the side walls; and at the end of the passage another portcullis. But the most interesting thing about this gatehouse is the way in which the whole approach is covered by scientifically disposed battlements, one above the other. First, the roof and turrets of the barbican; then, rising behind them, the walls and roof of the gatehouse, and then the gatehouse turrets, the first pair lower than the second, each shooting platform overlooking and supporting the one in front of it. The turrets of the gatehouse are joined by flying bridges of stone, so that the defenders had no need to go down to roof-level and up again in order to move from one turret to the other.

When you walk through the gate of a keep-and-bailey castle today, one like Warwick or Dover or Kenilworth or Corfe, you find a large empty area of cropped grass. When these castles were in use, what a different picture it would have been! The whole space would have been filled with buildings, mostly of timber, but some of stone. Against the walls of the bailey you would see lean-to shelters, some open in front and some completely closed in, stables, kennels for the hounds, *byres*, workshops of all kinds for masons, carpenters, armorers, blacksmiths (for, make no mistake, an armorer was a highly skilled specialist, not a blacksmith), stores for hay and straw like Dutch barns, dwellings for the army of castle servants and hangers-on, open-air kitchens, a large mess-room, stone mews for the falcons, a chapel, and a great hall, more airy and luxurious than the hall in the keep to be used in the long days of peace. Instead of grass, the ground would be of hard-packed earth, or cobbles or even pavement — or, in some lesser

Diagrams showing one method of working drawbridges.

(A) A drawbridge in the open, as in the barbican at Arques. The bridge is fastened by chains to two great horizontal beams, each pivoted on the upright beam. The chains to the end of the bridge are fastened to the outer ends of the beams, and there is a heavy weight at the inner end of each to act as a counterpoise to the weight of the bridge. These weighted ends are drawn down by chains attached to winches. Because of the counterbalance afforded by the weights the bridge can easily be raised and lowered by two men

(B) This shows a drawbridge in front of a gatehouse worked in the same way. The inner, weighted ends of the beams pass through holes in the wall, only the outer half projecting. When the bridge is raised, the beams set back into the slots in the wall above the gateway; similarly the drawbridge itself sets back into a recess in the front of the gateway. Thus when the bridge is raised, both it and the beams are flush with the outer surface of the wall. Some drawbridges are worked more simply by means of chains passing from the outer end of the bridge, through holes in the gatehouse wall to winches inside, but this method requires more power to lift the bridge.

castles, probably a quagmire of mud. And instead of groups of tourists and people picnicking in the shelter of the ruins, there would be a great bustle and coming-and-going of working people going about their everyday jobs. Cooking would be continual; there would be constant feeding, watering, and exercising of horses, movement of cattle in to be milked and out to graze; armorers and blacksmiths would be busy repairing harness for the garrison and making ironwork for the castle, shoeing horses, repairing carts and wagons — an endless hubbub of busy-ness. And the huntsmen and verderers would be constantly busy, for there was an army of animals, hounds and hawks and horses to be cared for, trained, and exercised for hunting. Every day hunting parties would be out after deer or small game like hares and rabbits and, on special occasions, wild boar, while others would take their falcons and go after all kinds of birds. Hunting and hawking, admittedly one of the chief pastimes of the upper ranges of feudal society, was much more of an essential part of everyday life than we might think. With so many mouths to feed, it was vital to get as much game for the pot as possible.

Though the keep-and-bailey castle was the most common all through the Middle Ages, by no means are all the castles in England or on the Continent of this pattern. This is because so often during the 13th century castles were greatly modified by additions and alterations to keep pace with new developments in siegecraft and in accordance with new ideas in defensive design. Richard the Lionhearted, for instance, was an accomplished military engineer; he put many new ideas into practice, altering some existing castles such as the Tower of London, and embodying all his new thoughts in the great castle at Les Andelys in Normandy, his famous "Chateau Gaillard," the castle that he boasted he could hold even if its walls were made of butter. It was in fact taken only a few years later by the King of France after a not very long siege, but it fell as so many castles did because of treachery from within.

Many old castles, then, were enlarged during this

One of the towers of the Chateau of Sully-sur-Loire, showing the machicolations round its top, and along the top of the wall. Here the old roofs are still in place as they were in the 14th century.

century; new towers and gatehouses, bastions and barbicans were built, and new features appeared. The old wooden hoardings, for instance, began to be replaced by stone *machicolations*. These did in fact more or less reproduce in stone the wooden, opendecked galleries, and this machicolation is one of the typical features of the 13th century castle.

But by the century's end an entirely new type of castle had developed in England, and several of them were built on new sites in Wales. After Edward I had conquered the principality in 1278 and 1282, he began to build a series of great castles on a new plan to hold down his conquest, as William I had done in England two hundred years before. But Edward's castles were very different from the motte-and-bailey, earthwork and stockade castles of his predecessors. Their design was, very roughly, that a central keep or citadel was done away with, and the walls and towers of the bailey were greatly strengthened. At Conway and Carnarvon, the outer walls were almost as high as those of an old-style keep, while the flanking towers had become enormous. The encircling walls still enclosed two open courts or baileys, but these were smaller than in the older, more open castles. Conway and Carnarvon were built on irregular plans to conform to the sites they stood upon, but Harlech and Beaumaris were based on the concept of a rectangular enclosure with very high, strong walls and a great drum-tower at each corner, the whole vast building enclosed within a concentric wall with bastions. There is no space here to describe these great castles in detail, but this does at least describe the basic idea behind their design.

The same principle was in force in the design of the last real castle to be built in England — great walls linking corner towers. Late in the 14th century, new

This shows how the machicolations were built.

castles of this kind were built at Bodiam in Sussex, Nunney in Somerset, Bolton and Sheriff Hutton in Yorkshire, Lumley in Durham, and Queenborough in the Isle of Sheppey. The last was not quadrangular, but circular and on a completely concentric plan. This castle was totally destroyed by the Parliament in the English Civil War, and no trace of it remains; all we know of it is from old drawings. The domestic buildings inside these castles were no longer either built to stand free in the bailey or built against its walls, but were all incorporated into the structure itself, making for a much more logically arranged and luxurious dwelling.

After the end of the 14th century, the English castle declined into the fortified manor-house, where domestic care and convenience were much more important than defense. Many built during the 15th century kept to the rectangular plan, and most had wet moats (the old word now changed in its meaning); the only military-seeming feature was the twin-towered gatehouse. By the end of the century, castle building had ceased and the Englishman's castle had indeed become his home, for with the 16th century came the beginning of the great age of the English manor-house.

These remarks do not, of course, apply to Continental castles; there, social conditions were different. In Germany, especially, private war went on without ceasing until the end of the 16th century, and castles were still very much in use. In England, on the Welsh Marches and the Scottish Border, the need for defense and strength was still valid. On the Welsh Marches the old castles were needed in the 15th century; indeed, at this time a completely new one was built at Raglan in Monmouthshire. Very much on the pattern of Edward I's castles, it was built in the years around 1400 by Sir William ap Thomas, known as 'The Blue Knight of Gwent,' and by his son Sir William Herbert, later Earl of Pembroke. It has one very striking feature that the Edwardian castles lacked — a great free-standing tower, hexagonal in plan, built upon its own mound and surrounded by a moat and a bastioned wall. It stands on its own, a

An aerial view of Harlech Castle. This is one of the great castles built in the time of Edward I, and shows the massive combination of the great drum towers joined in a rectangular plan by very high walls. The whole castle has in a way become a vast keep, with the gatehouse greatly enlarged and forming the most important building in the whole design. Before the main gatehouse with its huge towers is a much smaller one. There is a long bridge over the ditch, with a drawbridge (now of course a solid bridge) set at a slight angle at the inner end. There is a wall surrounding the outer edge of the ditch (the 'counterscarp') and another crowning the steep rocky sides of the inner bank. This castle is built on a high rocky hill, and the only possible approach for an assault is from the side you are looking at. You can imagine how difficult it would be to force a way across the counterscarp, then across the ditch, then up the rocky bank and the wall on top, then up and over the main wall – all the time being shot at from the walls and towers above you. All the domestic buildings at Harlech are in the block behind the main gate.

castle in its own right, in front of the main castle. It was known as 'The Yellow Tower of Gwent'.

This was a late example of new building in a region where a certain amount of warfare was to be expected, but in the border country of the North, warfare was endemic. There was no end to the cattle-lifting raids and forays of the Scots, and the counter-raids of the English. Every manor, every farm, had to be a castle. As a result, all over this country were built small castles, called *peels*. They consisted of a simple tower, grim and solid, in a small bailey which in most cases was no more than a yard, surrounded by a high, plain, un-crenellated wall. Most of these peels were farms, and when the raiders came into in sight, the owner and his family and farm-laborers would bolt for the shelter of the peel, driving their stock into the yard. If the Scots took the trouble to stop and batter the wall down, the castle inhabitants took refuge in the tower, driving the cattle into the basement and going themselves into the upper floor. But the Scots rarely bothered. They were always in a hurry to get on, get as much loot as possible, and get home.

The great Age of the Castle corresponded almost exactly with the Age of Chivalry — the 11th to the 15th centuries. Warfare, even private warfare, in the 15th century had become quite businesslike, much more modern, with more nastiness and less glamor than formerly it had, and the development of cannon had made even the strongest castle vulnerable as it had never been before. Yet it is curious that two hundred years after the last castles had been built in England, when many were deserted and falling into ruin, they came into their own again during the Civil War of 1642-49. Several stood long sieges, pounded by cannon far more powerful than those used in the 15th century, and none fell by direct assault.

The Castle Besieged

In war, the purpose of a castle was two-fold. It must be a place in which the leading men of a district could defend themselves against the attacks of their foes, but equally important was the fact that it was a place these same men could burst out of, to attack any force that came within range of them. No commander with any sense would risk marching his force past a hostile castle; he could rarely know whether it was held in strength by a garrison large and strong enough to take the offensive or by only two or three men-at-arms, a dozen archers, and the servants. He might, assuming it to be weakly held, pass it by only to be fallen upon by a strong force; so he would always tend to play safe and either stop to besiege it or give it a very wide berth.

There were only two ways of taking possession of a castle if it was defended — by battering a way in across the barriers of its defenses or by starving it out. Well, there was a third way — bribing someone inside to open the gate — but that does not concern us here. To sit down before a castle in regular siege

91

took a lot of time, and required many men and a train of siege engines. Often it was only possible to make a quick and violent assault in the hope of breaking in, for not many medieval armies marched with siege machines in their baggage train. Where such an assault was attempted, it was a matter of rushing forward, preferably at two or three places simultaneously to distract and divide the garrison, getting somehow across the moat, hoisting long ladders against the walls, getting as many men up them as fast as possible, hacking a way off the ladders on to the wall and through the embrasures of the parapet, then getting possession of one or more towers and so gaining the bailey. Then of course there would still be the keep to take; no scaling-ladder would reach its battlement, and unless the doorway and the forebuilding could be rushed while the garrison was still trying to defend parts of the bailey, or the door itself burnt down, even an assault that carried the bailey would be unable to take the castle.

Such an assault would be beaten off by successive means of defense. First, the defenders would try to stop or at least harass the attackers by means of arrows, bolts, sling-stones, and probably great darts and stones hurled from the castle's own engines. When the attack got to the foot of the bailey wall, the hot oil, water, lime, and so on would come into use, being poured through the openings in the hoarding or through the machicolations. When the ladders were reared against the wall, the defenders would try to push them away with long poles with forked ends. You can imagine that it would not have been at all easy to push away a ladder thirty feet long (about 9 meters), made of heavy timber, with fifteen or so armored men on it, set against the wall at an angle of about sixty degrees, with a pole pushed against its very top. The weight opposed to the pole would be tremendous. Of course, if the attackers placed their ladders at too steep an angle, they would be more easily overbalanced, as they would be if their lower ends were not firmly placed. Imagine yourself in the nightmare frenzy of an assault under a defended wall; you are showered with flaming oil; arrows and stones whistle down around you as you struggle to hold a great ladder erect. You stand on a sloping, muddy ground with a ditch probably full of deep water just behind you. There are dead men under your feet, and your comrades fall round you, some silent, some screaming with pain; your armor is slimy with hot oil, agonizing where it seeps into the joints or through the rings of your mail; every time you and your comrades manage to get the top of the ladder against the wall, it is pushed away. But you struggle on, and at last it settles in place at a good angle. Now your hands are free; you snatch out your weapons, sword or axe or mace, drag your shield round from your back, and with your men hurl yourself against the ladder, pressing it against the wall by your weight, holding your shield above you, trying frantically to hold the ladder and your sword at the same time as you climb. Stones and arrows thump and rattle on your shield and helmet; you go up as fast as you can to get to grips with the defenders on the wall and out of this hideous rain of missiles. Then you get level with the parapet. You are the leading man on your ladder; there seem to be dozens of warriors crowded into the embrasure before you, hacking and thrusting at you, doing everything they can to cut you down, overbalance you from your precarious stand on the ladder, and send you dashing thirty feet or more to join the broken bodies below. There are men behind you, stout comrades you can rely on, but not one of them can do a thing to help you. Only when you force a way on to the wall and clear a space can they come up to support you. Once you are on the rampart, there is really only one way down for you — either in victory down the stair in a tower, out into the bailey; or in defeat, thrown back over into the moat.

Such an assault was a desperate business, more difficult and hazardous for the attack than the defense, and when it was attempted as an isolated event, it was generally a failure. But when an attack on a broken-down wall came after the long preparation of a regular siege, it could be different.

There were three ways of breaking the walls of castles, each of them often employed in succession or simultaneously. The first was to batter a breach from a distance by casting great stones against the wall from stone throwing machines, which were called *petrariae* or simply *engines*. The second method was to use battering-rams, bores, or picks to make a great hole in the lower part of a wall to bring the top part down. The third was to undermine the wall with a tunnel, usually starting some distance from the wall, with its entrance carefully camouflaged so that the defenders could not see the miners digging. When the tunnel reached the wall, a large chamber — the mine proper — was dug below the foundations. As it was hollowed out, great props of timber were put in to prevent the whole thing from collapsing upon the miners. When the mine was big enough, a lot of brushwood and other objects were brought in, well soaked in fat and grease, and set on fire. A single man could be left to start the fire and see that it got going before he escaped along the tunnel, though this must have been a hazardous business because of the suffocating effect of the smoke. When the props burned through, the tower or section of wall above the mine fell in.

There were counter-measures that the garrison could take to hinder these forms of attack. Against the hurtling stones there was little that could be done in the way of direct defense; counterattack was the only means. Castles had their own petrariae from which their garrisons used to hurl stones in turn against the engines of their foes, often being able to break them up. Sometimes they shot barrels of *Greek fire*, a partly explosive and fiercely burning compound — a bit like modern napalm — the composition of which is now forgotten. Many besieging engines were destroyed in this way. A far more glamorous method of getting rid of engines was for a small party to sally out from the castle and set fire to them personally. In this way many splendid feats of arms were performed. The ram or bore was harder to combat. The defenders could let down a great mat made of hurdles or anything else they had handy to make a sort of super shock-absorbing fend-off, but such a thing seldom lasted long as the ram would soon batter it through even if the attackers were unable to sever the ropes by which it was hung from the parapet. Another trick was to lower a great beam with a forked end; the fork (in theory) was dropped over the neck of the ram, thus immobilizing it. But in practice this must have been almost impossible to achieve. Just imagine trying to lower a great twenty-foot beam (about 7 meters), hung on ropes, swaying about as it must, over the end of another beam or tree-trunk swinging backwards and forwards far below you — remembering that you would have to lean out through an embrasure to do it, where you would be exposed all the time to the bolts and arrows of the attackers.

Against the mine the only defense was a counter-mine — that is, a tunnel dug from your side of the wall to meet the tunnel of the attackers — depending upon your knowledge of the whereabouts of the mine. By the time the attackers' tunnel got dangerously near it was not difficult to know its location, for it was impossible to disguise the vibrations of the miner's picks under the wall. The defenders constantly listened for their sinister sounds. There are many stories of fierce underground fights by lantern-light in the murky darkness of mine-tunnels. Sometimes, when the counter-mine had actually entered the mine-chamber, the parties of sappers, after a skirmish, would be withdrawn to allow their knightly superiors to come down and engage in most worshipful feats of arms. Henry V went into a mine under the walls of Melun when he was besieging it in 1421 and fought with the Governor of the town, the Sire de Barbazan.

Sometimes when the besiegers had finished their mine chamber, they would call out to the commander of the garrison. When he came to the wall, or hung out of a window, he was told his castle was undermined and asked to surrender. On some occasions he refused to believe he was undermined; then he would be invited to come down, under a flag of truce, and see for himself. This was an eminently sensible thing to do, for no besieger wanted to waste more time, effort, or lives than was necessary, and since he often wanted the castle himself, or for his lord or king, he wouldn't damage it if he could help it. When the defending commander had seen that resistance was futile, the mine was filled in again and all was well.

The engines used for these forms of attack were very simple in principle and had changed little since the days of the ancient Assyrians in about 700 B.C. It is hard to say precisely how these were made, for the various descriptions of them in the medieval chronicles are very vague; however, we can get a general idea. First was the *trebuchet*, for throwing the heaviest stones. This was made of a framework, often with small wheels to enable it to be moved, supporting two great upright posts. Working on a pivot between these posts was a long arm; the pivot was set well to one end of it, so that one end was long and the other shorter. To the end of the long arm was fastened a leather bag like the pouch of a sling, while to the short arm was attached a great weight. In preparing to shoot, the long end was pulled right down, raising the weight into the air, and fastened. Then a rock was loaded into the pouch. A peg or wedge was pulled out of the fastening of the arm, releasing it; then the weight of the short end crashed down, whipping the loaded long end through the arc of a circle and flinging the stone with tremendous force against its target.

An older and perhaps slightly less powerful machine was the *mangon* or *mangonel*. This worked by the principle of torsion, that is, twisting. The same pair of upright posts held the same sort of long arm, but in the mangonel the arm was secured right at the bottom of the posts, and the short end was much shorter. The arm was pushed through a web of twisted cords, and at its end was a large spoon-shaped bowl, or a pouch as on a trebuchet. To load it, the end was pulled right down and fastened with a rope with a release-catch. Then the web of ropes was twisted tighter and tighter by a sort of vertical capstan on the axle of the pivot. When it was as tight as it could go, the capstan was secured by wedges or a catch. Then, to shoot, the catch at the end was released; the twisted ropes sprang back, the spoon or pouch at the end of the arm was thrown violently upward, to be stopped by a cross-beam, padded in the middle, and the stone, barrel of Greek fire, or other missile was hurled forward. If you take an ordinary ruler, hold one end in your left hand, and pull back the other end with a lump of chewing-gum or paper on it and let it go, you will be using a mangonel. If you let your rule hit something, at the point where it reaches a vertical position, your lump of gum will go farther and hit its target harder.

Another form of artillery was a *ballista,* which was like an enormous cross-bow on a pivoted stand. The Romans used them in the manner of light field guns. They had no wheels, but were mounted on vertical stands about four feet (1.25 meters) from the ground. The frame of the machine — the part corresponding to the stock of a cross-bow — was pivoted on the top of the stand so that it could traverse in a complete half-circle and could be elevated or depressed as necessary. These could be worked by only two or three men, shooting quite fast, and could be protected by a shield fitted in front of the bow, just like a shield on an old-fashioned field-gun. These of course were anti-personnel weapons, used from long range to pick off defenders who exposed themselves on the walls, or to shoot fire-tipped bolts to burn roofs or hoardings and the houses in the bailey.

The *ram* was slung on ropes from the cross-beams and between the uprights. Whenever possible, the head was made of solid iron, with a point to it. Its purpose was simply to bash and batter at the stones of the wall, but as it had to be dragged right up to the wall its use involved much preliminary work. Part of the ditch had to be filled in, and the whole machine dragged forward under fire. Since men would have to work at it, swinging the ram for hours on end, they had to be protected by making a great shed to contain the whole thing. This, to strengthen it, and in an effort to make it fireproof, was covered with raw hides and sometimes sheets of iron.

The *pick* worked on the same principle, only instead of a great heavy trunk for battering, the tree used would be long and slender, with a long, sharp iron spike at its end. This was used with more finesse, picking away at the cracks between the stones of the wall. The *bore,* also working in a penthouse, was like a pick only it was used in the manner of a gigantic drill, boring away the mortar between the stones.

Another machine that was commonly used to assault the wall was a great moveable tower, which could be dragged up to the wall. There were several stages or floors in the tower, with ladders connecting them, and the front of the upper floor was a sort of large iron-faced drawbridge. Each floor would be filled with men-at-arms; when the tower was near enough to the wall, the drawbridge was lowered, and a stream of men from the upper floor would rush across on to the wall, followed up by the men from the lower stages. Once such a tower actually got near enough to the wall for the drawbridge to reach across to it, the defenders had a rather poor chance; but until its fighting men had gotten on to the wall, the tower's position was very dangerous. It presented a large target, moving horribly slowly, to the castle's engines; their ballistae, at such close range, could shoot great iron bolts right through its walls of hide and wood. Though it would have been well soaked before it started, by the time it reached the wall the

A trebuchet. These were made in various sizes, some quite small, others even bigger than this. The short end carried a great weight, usually a huge basket filled with rocks; the long end, with a sling on it to contain the missile, was pulled right down by ropes working on a windlass. When this end was released, the weight at the other end came down and the sling swung up and released its missile – a large stone, generally, but sometimes a dead horse – a medieval form of germ warfare – or on a few grim occasions a prisoner or a hostage.

sun would have dried it, and it was susceptible to Greek fire or burning oil. The poor wretches who had to haul it across the uneven ground and the filled-in section of the ditch were exposed all the time, and their losses must have been heavy. To the knights and men-at-arms inside, the two or three hours' journey (for it could take as long as that) must

A mangonel. This performed the same function as the trebuchet, but is worked by a different principle. One end of the long arm is held by a web of twisted ropes, the other has a sort of spoon bowl to put the missile in. The arm is then pulled down by rope and winch, and the twisted ropes are wound very tight by another winch. Then the free end is released.

have been a nightmare.

Another use of the tower (or *belfry* as it was afterwards called) was to station it at some distance from the wall, and use it as a look-out post or to fill it with archers and cross-bowmen who could shoot down on to the tops of the castle walls. Henry III did this when he besieged Bedford Castle in 1224; its effect was such that the defenders never dared to take any of their armor off, so exposed were they to the shot of their opponents.

Various nicknames were given to these engines. The penthouses covering rams were often called *cats* or *sows* while the pick was called a *mouse*. At the siege of Kenilworth in 1265 the belfry filled with archers (like Henry III's at Bedford forty-one years before) was called 'The Bear', and a common nickname for the petrariae was *malvoisin* (bad neighbor). Most engines were given names, sometimes by the attackers who used them, often by the defenders who

A ballista. This is just a huge cross-bow on a revolving stand, and shoots great iron bolts.

suffered from them.

It is tempting to imagine that the garrison of the 13th-century castle would have been very large; one thinks of bailey walls crowded with fighting men

A cat, or sow. The battering-ram is protected by a long shed, which is covered with raw hides to protect its timbers from fire.

along the whole perimeter, but in fact it was not so. The peace-time garrison of most castles, even the great royal ones like Corfe or Dover or Oxford, only consisted of half-a-dozen knights, perhaps twenty other men-at-arms, fourteen crossbowmen, a chaplain, and sundry servants such as cooks, carpenters, etc. A smaller castle would have even fewer — one knight, four men-at-arms, three crossbowmen. Even in war the numbers of castle garrisons seem incredibly small. The Pipe Roll for 1174 mentions only twenty knights at Oxford and ten knights and forty men-at-arms at Wark; this was in a year when Henry II was battling in England against his rebellious sons. When John rebelled against his brother Richard I, when that lion-hearted monarch was a prisoner of war in Germany in 1193, the Pipe Roll gives a total garrison of only seventy-five men for both Norwich — a very large castle — and Canterbury. In 1215 when John besieged Rochester Castle, his force was opposed by only one hundred knights and men-at-arms, some crossbowmen, and various servants; a year later Dover was held against the besieging force of the French Prince Louis by a much larger force. Roger of Wendover says there were one hundred and forty knights and many men-at-arms and others. But then Dover was an exceptionally important and large castle. The fact that castles could be held for such long periods against such strong besieging forces shows how extremely efficient their defenses

Diagram of the ram in action at the foot of a wall

were. In 1216 Odiham in Hampshire held out for
two weeks, defended by only three knights and ten
men-at-arms. Centuries later, Corfe Castle held out
for even longer against a Parliament army, complete
with quite efficient cannon; it was defended by an
old woman (Lady Mary Bankes), a few old retainers,
and some servant-girls. The Parliamentary leader
only took it because one of the servants lost his nerve
and opened a gate from inside.

Finally, let us look at the accounts of some sieges.
The first describes the taking of the motte-and-bailey
castle of le Puiset in France in 1111. It was besieged
by the forces of King Louis the Fat and was held by
Hugh of le Puiset, its Lord. The garrison began
operations by coming out and trying to drive the
King's forces off before he had settled down in a
regular siege, but this failed and they went back
behind their palisades. The next move was by the
besiegers; they sent a detachment off, led by Count
Theobald of Chartres, to try to storm the bailey wall
round at the back. This failed too, partly because the
bank was high and steep, but mainly by reason of a
fierce, sudden mounted attack made by the garrison.
The King's men, suffering considerable losses, were
cut up and thrown into the ditch, while the horsemen
rode happily back into the castle. Then after a while
the main part of the besieging force, worked up to a
fighting frenzy by a priest, delivered a massed attack
across the ditch. They stormed up the earth bank to
the palisade and, in spite of all that the defenders
could do, they hacked and trampled a gap in it,

A belfry, a large moveable tower which is dragged up to the wall, full of fighting men. When it gets near enough, a drawbridge is dropped over the parapet and the men inside the belfrey swarm across on to the wall. The sides of the tower are covered with hides to lessen the likelihood of its being burnt.

wrenching the great logs away, and burst into the bailey. Hugh of le Puiset and the survivors of the garrison bolted for the mound itself, the central stronghold of the castle, but they had lost many men in the fight for the bailey. They could neither defend the motte and the tower nor escape to the open country, so they soon gave in.

Here we have a good instance of the active means a garrison could use in its defense, making fierce and sudden sorties. Even in a castle, the best form of defense was usually to attack.

The siege of Rochester Castle in 1215, when it was held by rebellious barons against King John, gives one of the rare examples of a keep actually being broken into and carried by storm. Getting past the outer defenses, the besiegers were held up by the massive square tower. But the King's miners managed to drive a tunnel under one of the corners, and dug a great mine chamber. This was propped up with timber and filled with brushwood in the usual way. A royal writ addressed to the King's Justiciar, Hubert de Burgh, still survives: "We command you that with all haste, by day and by night, you send us forty bacon pigs of the fattest and those less good for eating to bring fire under the tower..." Why pigs? They were slaughtered when they reached the castle, cut up, and rendered for bacon fat. This was then smeared thickly over the timbers in the mine, and poured over the brushwood. You can imagine how the mine must have burned. The whole corner turret came down, and the King's men poured into the keep; but then they came up against the cross-wall. The defenders retreated behind this, and held out for a few more days.

If you ever see Rochester keep, look at the four corner turrets. Three are the original square ones, but one is larger and round. For many years after 1215 the keep stood shattered, one corner in ruins; but Henry III built a new tower, and there it remains. Some may say it is there because Henry III had it built, but it's really on account of those forty fat pigs.

The best example of the successful taking of a castle is the capture of Bedford Castle in 1224. It was held, in defiance of the young King Henry III, by one of John's old mercenary captains, Fawkes de Breaute. Fawkes himself was away when the siege began, but his brother and his wife were in the castle, and held it for him against the full forces of the King. As a beginning, the garrison was solemnly excommunicated; then the siege engines were set in position. We read that a trebuchet and two mangonels were set up on the east, two mangonels on the west, one mangonel on the north, and another on the south to shoot against the keep. Two great belfrys were raised, overlooking the walls, from which the crossbowmen continuously kept watch on the garrison so that they had to keep their armor on and their heads down all the time. Then day after day the garrison were given no rest from the showers of bolts and the pounding of great stones against their walls. They had no intention of surrendering; they believed that if they held out, their Lord Fawkes de Breaute would

come to their help. They defended themselves
fiercely, killing Lord Richard de Argentan, six
knights, and over two hundred men-at-arms and
laborers on the engines. The King saw that there
would be a long siege; he became very bitter about
it, and swore that he would hang all the garrison if
he took the castle.

Taken it was, in the end, in four attacks. First the
barbican fell. Then, losing several men, the besiegers
took the bailey, and in it most of the castle's stores
and provisions of corn, pigs, and cattle, as well as the
horses and harness, a great deal of armor, and
crossbows. Now they were up against the tough core
of the defense — the towers and walls on the mound
and the keep itself. Here the miners got to work; they
brought down a length of the great wall (like a
shell-keep) encircling the top of the mound. Now the
attackers were inside the inner bailey, faced only by
the keep, after a long and hard assault where some
men were killed and ten more captured and carried
off into the keep. Then the miners went to it again,
and "on the Vigil of the Assumption, towards Ves-
pers" — that is, at about four o'clock on the afternoon
of August 14 — the mine was fired. The smoke
poured into the inner rooms of the keep, suffocating
the exhausted, starving defenders, and the tower
sank upon its foundations with great cracks appear-
ing in the walls. It was no use trying any more. The
women (including Fawkes' wife) and the prisoners
were sent out, and the remainder of the garrison
hauled up the royal banner in token of surrender.

The next morning they were brought before the King; they were absolved from their excommunication, and six of the leaders were hanged with William, Fawkes' brother.

There are many surviving records that tell us of the arrangements that had to be made to organize this siege. Engines had to be carted from Lincoln and all across Oxfordshire from Northampton; others had to be built on the spot out of timber felled in the woods of Northamptonshire and carted to Bedford. (The monks of Warden complained when the Royal foresters cut down their trees.) Carpenters were called up; the Constable of Windsor was ordered to provide horses for Master Thomas and others and their tools, "so that they shall be able to travel to us by day and by night as swiftly as they can and not tarry." Others were sent from Lincoln and London. From London too, as well as from Cambridge and Southampton, came ropes and cables for the engines. Hides to make the slings and to cover the belfrys and cats came from Northampton, and tallow to lubricate the machinery was sent from London. The Sheriffs of Bedfordshire and Northamptonshire were told "to send to us, without delay, at Bedford all the quarrymen and stonecutters in your jurisdiction, with levers, sledges, and petrariae." Roger de Clifford, Constable of St. Briavels, sent miners from Hereford and the Forest of Dean. Crossbowmen came from London, and bolts for them were sent in the thousands. The Bailiffs of Northampton were ordered, "as you love us and our honor, that you cause to be made, both by day and by night, by all the smiths in the town that are skilled in the art, four thousand quarrels, well barbed and well flighted..." and to send them to Bedford. Fifteen thousand bolts were sent up from Corfe, too.

These items give some idea of the kind of job it was to lay formal siege to a castle. When the King himself was present, there were extras. All his colorful and emblazoned tents and pavilions were sent up from London in carts, with all his arms and personal comforts as well as such luxuries as cinnamon, ginger, pepper, saffron, almonds, and great quantities of wine of all kinds. When it was all over, everything was packed up and sent back; the engines were dismantled, the parts sent back to the Tower of London and to Northampton, and the carpenters, miners, stone workers, leather workers, and laborers were able to return to their ordinary jobs. Bedford Castle was slighted, that is, all its defenses were broken down and made useless, and Fawkes de Breaute, deserted by his friends and his wife, went into exile.

Many of the castles in England today are very ruinous, more so than the passage of time seems to warrant. This is often because they were deliberately slighted, wholly or partly. But like England's ruined abbeys, which might still be in a condition as good as that of the great cathedrals if it had not been for Henry VIII's dissolution of the monasteries, many castles survived in good order until, in the Great Civil War of 1642–49, they were held, like Corfe, for the

King. In order that those that had been captured should not be used against the Parliament again, and to prevent many others from being so used, their bailey walls, towers, gatehouses, curtain walls, and keeps were blown up. The shattered ruins of Corfe Castle in Dorset, once one of the proudest possessions of the English crown, are at the same time a monument to the heroic defense of old Lady Bankes and her servants and to the strength of the castle. For if you look at the scattered fragments of yellowish-grey stonework that litter the great natural mound of Corfe, you can see how strong and solid the work is. Had it not been blown to pieces, it would have stood almost untouched until today, like some of the other great castles that have been more fortunate.

Glossary

Allure: a protected walkway along the top of a stone castle wall.

Almonry: the office or building from which alms (money, food, clothing) are distributed to the poor.

Ashlar: a square building stone used for facing.

Bailey: 1-the defensive wall surrounding the outer courtyard of a castle. 2- the courtyard itself.

Ballista: a large cross-bow-like weapon on a pivoted stand, worked by two or three men.

Barbican: a defensive fortification at the gate of a castle, usually consisting of two long, high parallel walls built out from the gate; the purpose of the barbican was to force attackers into a narrow passage where they could more easily be shot at.

Bastion: a tower projecting out from the bailey wall.

Battlement: a low wall with open spaces for shooting.

Belfry: in medieval warfare, a moveable tower with several floors that could be used as a look-out post or a station for archers or, being filled with men-at-arms, dragged with much difficulty and danger right up against a castle wall to mount an assault.

Besagew: an armor plate protecting an open area, as at the elbow or armpit.

Billets: a soldier's lodging.

115

Bore: like a pick; a slender, spike-tipped tree trunk, worked like a giant drill to loosen the mortar between stones in a castle wall.

Bowyer: a maker of bows.

Brattice: see "hoarding."

Brazier: a metal container to hold burning coals.

Bulwark: a defensive wall.

Burgess: a citizen of a burg or borough.

Buttress: a structure built against a wall to support or reinforce it.

Byre: a barn or shed.

Cat: (also "sow") a nickname for the large, moveable shed, covered with animal hides and sometimes sheets of iron, used to house and protect the various rams, picks, and bores and the men who worked them during a siege.

Chaplet: a wreath or garland for the head.

Chevalier: (French) a knight.

Citadel: the central fortress of a castle containing storerooms and living quarters; the keep.

Constable: the highest ranking official in residence in a castle.

Coronation: a ceremony to crown a new king or queen.

Counterscarp: the outer rim of the ditch surrounding a castle.

Courser: a swift horse.

Crenellation: an opening or indentation along the top of a castle wall.

Dais: a raised platform on which a throne, for instance, would sit.

Diaper: to ornament with a pattern of small, constantly repeated figures, such as squares or diamonds.

Doge: the chief magistrate of either of the former republics of Genoa and Venice.

Donjon: a tower keep.

Embrasures: open spaces along a parapet.

Engine: in medieval times, any of the various large war machines, such as the mangonel or trebuchet.

Exchequer: the funds in a national treasury.

Farrier: a person that shoes horses.

Fee: (also "fief") a piece of land given in return for military service.

Fletcher: an arrowmaker.

Frieze: a painted or sculpted band of decoration around a building or room.

Garderobe: a latrine in a medieval castle.

Garrison: the defenders stationed at a castle.

Gauntlet: a heavy glove worn to protect the hand in combat.

Gesso: a prepared surface of plaster or plaster-like material for painting.

Gild: to coat with a thin layer of gold.

Glazier: a glass-cutter.

Granary: a room or building for storing grain.

Greek fire: a partly explosive and fiercely burning compound of now unknown composition used in medieval warfare.

Habiliments: articles of clothing.

Helm: a helmet.

Herald: an official messenger.

Hoarding: a roofed walkway projecting out along the tops of castle walls or towers, with openings in the floor through which repellants could be dropped on attackers.

Honor: all the land owned by a lord.

Indenture: a written contract or agreement.

Joust: a combat between two knights on horseback using lances.

Keep: the strongest and central tower of a castle.

Knight errant: a "wandering knight," one who swore no permanent allegiance to a lord, but traveled around seeking adventure anywhere.

Loggia: a covered walkway or porch opened to the air on at least one side.

Mace: a heavy, spiked, armor-breaking club.

Machicolation: an opening in the floor through which boiling oil or water, rocks, etc. could be dropped on attackers.

Malvoisin: (literally, "bad neighbor") a nickname for the war machines called petrariae.

Mangonel: (or mangon) a machine for throwing large stones and darts. The short end of a long arm was pushed through a web of cords that acted as a pivot between two upright supporting posts; the long end of the arm, with a large bowl or pouch attached and loaded, was fastened down, the web of ropes twisted tightly, the arm released, thrown upward as the ropes sprung back, and stopped at the height of its arc by a padded cross-beam as the projectile shot forward.

Mercenary: a person who fights in an army for pay.

Merlon: a section of the parapet wall between embrasure openings.

Meurtriere: meaning "murder hole," a hole in the roof of an entrance passage for pouring water through to douse fires below, or for dropping repellants onto attackers.

Mews: a caged enclosure for hawks or falcons.

Michaelmas: festival celebrated on September 29th.

Moat: the ditch encircling a castle, sometimes filled with water.

Motte: the great mound of earth in early castles on which the central keep was built.

Mouse: a nickname for the pick.

Nave: the main part of a church between the side aisles.

Oratory: a small chapel.

Page: a boy training for knighthood.

Palisade: a wall consisting of pointed wooden spikes set firmly in the ground.

Parapet: a protecting stone wall built atop the thick main wall of a castle.

Peel: a small castle house in northern England built to defend against Scottish raiders.

Pennon: distinctive flag on the lance of a knight.

Petraria: a stone-throwing machine.

Pick: a weapon consisting of a long, slender tree trunk, cut and fitted with a sharp iron spike at one end, used to pick away at the cracks between stones in a castle wall.

Pilaster: a supporting column.

Pilgrimage: a journey to a shrine or holy place.

Plummet: a pointed stick of lead used like a pencil.

Portcullis: a heavy, grilled wooden or metal gate, with spikes along the bottom, which could be raised and lowered to open or block the castle entrance.

Posse Comitatus: a body of men in a county who could be called into service by the authorities when their help was needed to preserve the peace.

Quarrel: a square-headed bolt or arrow used with a cross-bow.

Ram: a large, cut tree trunk, often fitted with a pointed iron head, used to batter down a castle wall during a siege.

Rampart: the parapet-topped embankment of earth encircling a castle.

Sapper: a mine- or tunnel-digger (from "sap": a trench or tunnel for undermining an enemy position).

Scarp: the steep bank on the inside of the ditch, or moat, surrounding a castle, formed from the dirt dug to make the moat.

Shell-keep: Sometimes, when an old timber castle was being rebuilt with stone, instead of erecting a great tower keep on the motte, the timber palisade around the motte would be replaced by a high stone wall, within which all the living quarters and storerooms were built; this whole wall and enclosed area was called a shell-keep.

Sow: (also "cat") a nickname for the moveable shed, covered with raw hides and sometimes sheets of iron, used to house and protect the various rams, picks, and bores and the men who worked them during a siege.

Squire: a candidate for knighthood who acts as an attendant for a knight.

Steward: an official responsible for the preparing and serving of food in a royal household.

Stockade: an enclosure made of stakes driven into the ground side by side.

Tourelle: (French) a turret.

Trappings: ornamental coverings for a horse.

Trebuchet: a moveable war engine for throwing heavy stones, consisting of a long arm pivoting near one end between two upright posts. A leather pouch at the long end accepted the rock-missile while a great weight on the short end provided the power. The long end was pulled down, fastened, and loaded. When released, the short end dropped, whipping the long end with its loaded pouch around and propelling the stone toward the target.

Turret: a small tower at the corner of a castle wall.

Venery: hunting and general woodcraft arts.

Verderer: a judicial officer in the royal forests, like our forest rangers.

Wainscot: wood panels used to line interior walls of a residence.

Yeoman: an attendant or servant in a royal or noble household.

Index